GOD IN SOCIETY

GOD IN SOCIETY

Doing Social Theology in Scotland Today

Edited by

WILLIAM STORRAR and PETER DONALD

CENTRE FOR THEOLOGY AND PUBLIC ISSUES

NEW COLLEGE

THE UNIVERSITY OF EDINBURGH

SAINT ANDREW PRESS

First published in 2003 by
SAINT ANDREW PRESS
121 George Street
Edinburgh EH2 4YN

Copyright © the Contributors, 2003

ISBN 0 7152 0803 9

All rights reserved. No part of this publication may be reproduced
or transmitted in any form or by any means, electronic or mechanical,
including photocopying, recording, or information storage and retrieval
system, without permission in writing from the publisher. This book
is sold subject to the condition that it shall not, by way of trade or
otherwise, be lent, re-sold, hired out or otherwise circulated without
the publisher's prior consent.

The right of the Contributors to be identified as authors of this work has been
asserted in accordance with the Copyright, Designs and Patents Act 1988.

British Library Cataloguing in Publication Data
A catalogue record for this book is available from the British Library

Typeset in Sabon by Waverley Typesetters, Galashiels
Printed and bound in the United Kingdom by Bell & Bain Ltd, Glasgow

Let our three-voiced country sing in a new world.

Iain Crichton Smith,
from *The Makar's Court*

ESSAYS IN HONOUR OF

REV. DR ANDREW MORTON

ASSOCIATE DIRECTOR

CENTRE FOR THEOLOGY AND PUBLIC ISSUES

1994–2001

Contents

Part III

Doing Social Theology: Listening to Different Voices   123

Part IV

Doing Social Theology: Church Ways of Working   175

Note on the Extracts between Chapters

Shirley Williams, herself a Catholic, once referred to theology as embroidery. Others have talked of *stratospheric* theology, meaning devoid of social relevance. Even a theology which describes itself as social can sound esoteric. On the other hand, there are many artists and writers, at least in Scotland, who, without a theological interest as such, have been able to communicate to the population at large some hints of transcendence. The excerpts from poets and other writers interwoven between the chapters of this book, therefore, both reflect the society of which in Scotland we are a part and at the same time, it is hoped, stimulate the reader to make connections with the theological insights offered in this book.

WILLY SLAVIN

Contributors

Dr Marcella Althaus-Reid is Senior Lecturer in Theology and Christian Ethics at the University of Edinburgh. She teaches in the fields of liberation theology, feminist theology and theology and the global economy. Her research interests are in theology, sex, gender and politics.

Jeremy Balfour is the Parliamentary Officer for the Evangelical Alliance Scotland, liaising with the Scottish Parliament. He is a lawyer by background and has been active in electoral politics in Scotland.

Dr Graham Blount is the Scottish Churches' Parliamentary Officer, a new appointment since the establishment of the Scottish Parliament in 1999. He is a Church of Scotland minister.

Malcolm Cuthbertson is parish minister of Easterhouse St George's and St Peter's, Glasgow, and is currently engaged in research on folk religion and mission. He is also part-time lecturer at the International Christian College, Glasgow, on urban mission and community development issues.

Dr Peter Donald is a parish minister in Inverness. He represents the Church of Scotland on the Commission on Faith and Order of the World Council of Churches and also serves on the Church of Scotland's Panel on Worship.

Professor Duncan Forrester is Professor Emeritus of Christian Ethics and Practical Theology at the University of Edinburgh and was instrumental in the establishment of its Centre for Theology and Public Issues. He is a Church of Scotland minister.

Gerard Hand is parish priest of St Patrick's, Kilsyth, and Justice and Peace Advisor for the Roman Catholic Archdiocese of Edinburgh.

Alastair Hulbert was a mission partner of the Church of Scotland with the European Ecumenical Commission for Church and Society in Brussels during the 1990s. After serving as the Organising Secretary for the Centre for Theology and Public Issues at the University of Edinburgh, he is now Warden of Scottish Churches House, Dunblane.

Dr Andrew Morton is recently retired as Associate Director of the Centre for Theology and Public Issues in the University of Edinburgh. A Church of Scotland minister, he was at one time Community Affairs Secretary of the British Council of Churches and later Deputy General Secretary of the Church of Scotland Board of World Mission and Unity.

Professor George Newlands is Professor of Divinity in the University of Glasgow and is Principal of Trinity College.

Professor Nicholas Sagovsky was until recently the William Leech professorial research fellow in Applied Christian Theology in the department of Religious Studies in the University of Newcastle.

Norman Shanks is a Church of Scotland minister. He was Leader of the Iona Community from 1995 to 2002 and is currently a member of the Central Committee of the World Council of Churches and President of the Scottish Churches Open College.

Dr David Sinclair is the full-time Secretary of the Church of Scotland's Committee on Church and Nation, having previously worked as a parish minister.

Willy Slavin is a Catholic priest and psychologist. He is currently chaplain at the Royal Hospital for Sick Children, Glasgow.

Professor William Storrar holds the chair of Christian Ethics and Practical Theology in the University of Edinburgh, where he also directs the Centre for Theology and Public Issues. He is a Church of Scotland minister.

Acknowledgements

God in Society: Doing Social Theology in Scotland Today is the product of a group constituted by the Centre for Theology and Public Issues, a research centre within the School of Divinity, New College, at the University of Edinburgh since 1984. The group began as a theological monitoring reflection group on the various publications and events of the Centre, all of these in diverse ways trying to foster conversation between theologians and those at the directing or receiving end of public policy. In 1997, under the convenership of Dr William F. Storrar, the group took on the positive task of working towards the publication here in hand, both through plenary meetings and in sub-groups. Although in the end various individuals had the task of scribing, the interplay within the group and with other interested parties played a significant role. Therefore the Editors gladly acknowledge the insight and participation of Professor David Carr, Ms Julie Clague, Ms Mary Cullen, Professor Fred Edwards, Dr Alison Elliot, Dr Kevin Franz, Rev Alison Fuller, Professor Donald McLeod, Rev John McLuckie, Dr Lesley Orr Macdonald, Dr Michael Purcell, Ms Morag Ross, and any others accidentally omitted. The editors also wish to thank Alastair Hulbert for his invaluable and expert editorial assistance in preparing the manuscript for publication. Comments, of whatever length, arising from this publication will be gratefully received by the Organising Secretary of the Centre for Theology and Public Issues, at New College, The University of Edinburgh, Mound Place, Edinburgh, EH1 2LX, Tel. 0131 650 7991; e-mail: ctpi@ed.ac.uk The Centre gratefully acknowledges the generous support of the Christendom Trust in funding this project.

The Editors also wish to thank Ann Crawford, Richard Allen, Alison Fleming and colleagues at Saint Andrew Press for their professional support in publishing this book and launching our new joint series with the Centre for Theology and Public Issues, *Public Concerns*.

The Editors gratefully acknowledge permission from the following to reproduce in-copyright material:

'Christ of Scotland', in *Love Burning Deep* by Kathy Galloway, used by kind permission of SPCK.

'Scotland', by William Soutar, in *Poems*, ed. W. R. Aitken, published by Scottish Academic Press, reproduced courtesy of the Trustees of the National Library of Scotland.

'Why Scottish Philosophy Matters', by Alexander Broadie, reproduced courtesy of The Saltire Society.

'Proposals for a new Scottish Parliament', by Dennis Smith, in *Without Day*, ed. Alec Finlay, published by Pocketbooks, used by permission of the author.

'Alias MacAlias', by Hamish Henderson, published by Polygon, used by kind permission of Birlinn Press.

'Standing at the Edge', in *The Gift Half Understood: essays on a European journey* by Alastair Hulbert, used by kind permission of Melisende.

'A Drunk Man Looks at the Thistle', in *Complete Poems* by Hugh MacDiarmid, published by Scottish Academic Press. Reproduced courtesy of Carcanet Press.

'The Remapping of Scotland', by Kenneth White, used by kind permission of the Edinburgh International Book Festival.

'The Resurrection', from *The Myth of the Twin* by John Burnside, published by Jonathan Cape. Used by permission of The Random House Group Limited.

Personal reflection by Christopher Whyte, in the Anthology, *Across the Water: Irishness in modern Scottish writing*. Used by kind permission of Argyll Press.

'Crossing the Border', from *Collected Poems* by Norman MacCaig, published by Chatto & Windus. Used by permission of The Random House Group Limited.

'A Hymn which is not to Lenin', by Fearghas Mac-Fhionnlaigh, translated from the Gaelic, LAOIDH NACH EIL DO LENIN by the author, from *Scottish Religious Verse*, published by Saint Andrew Press. Reproduced by kind permission of the author.

Finally, the Editors and contributors to this volume wish to dedicate it to the Revd Dr Andrew R. Morton, in appreciation of his outstanding contribution to the work of the Centre for Theology and Public Issues, as its Associate Director 1994–2001; and in recognition of his lifetime of distinguished service to ecumenical social theology and witness.

Introduction

The sub-title of this book, *Doing Social Theology in Scotland Today*, fittingly describes the project behind the publication of these essays while also signalling clearly the limitations of whatever is achieved here. We hope that we have something to say – but it is not the last word. The authors offer their work in the hope of stimulating not only reflection but also dialogue that will continue, both within Scotland and further afield.

Doing

To unpick the sub-title is probably the most helpful and direct means of introduction. There is first the notion that we are about the 'doing' of theology. The theological task is more than an exercise in the study, important though academic reflection is. There is implied an active commitment, a living out of the wisdom; the word is alive. Therefore, as Christian theology takes shape, Christian faith is a starting point. When contributions are offered on the part of some churches, they come from those who themselves are active within those structures. As the impact of and aspirations surrounding the re-establishment of the Scottish parliament are explored, it is done by those who give time and energy to that institution in their life and work. In short, the doing of theology is not the task of an onlooker, however vital it may be to listen carefully to the outsider's perspective. Wisdom arises out of participation, and its most rigorous testing is through experience.

That said, there are clearly dangers in the 'doing' of theology as it has been described. If an active commitment to what truly matters promises a measure of integrity, it is also vulnerable to reinforcing blind spots. At worst, it can be fanatically misguided. Furthermore, there are very probably discrepancies between belief and practice. The ideas may be well stated but unrealistic or perhaps their execution shoddy or partial. The sins of hypocrisy, inconsistency and mere human weakness are all too likely. Within the parameters of this particular project, *God in Society*, the process has been to work jointly. Papers have been shared at various stages with the group and refined in the light of discussions. Latterly, a wider consultation exercise was held, to which others who had not been party to the earlier process were invited to read and to talk through the work produced. Although for practical reasons the papers are issued in the authors' own names and with each author taking individual responsibility for the language used, there has been a genuine attempt to tap collaborative wisdom and insight. In addition, the editors have linked closely with these chapters any questions remaining to be addressed – issues raised within discussions already heard. It is hoped very much that, in the reception of the whole book, others likewise committed, or at a distance, may feel encouraged to engage both with the arguments offered and the questions posed. The continued testing of insights will come through experience both prior to and subsequent to reflection.

Social Theology

Social theology within this project refers to that sphere of experience which both informs and tests the reflective process, namely the making of human community. The word becomes flesh in the context of social relations – church, parliament, bowling club, family, to name but a few. If an active commitment is presupposed, it is the commitment to community.

But what is 'the community'? The answer is not a simple one in our present-day context, when there are rhetorics of community often at odds one with another. If some uphold 'community values' or 'community well-being', others are entitled to ask 'whose community?' and 'whose well-being?' There is concern that appeal to the notion of community has become empty and devoid of content, or else is irredeemably imperialistic. Such serious question-marks cannot be avoided by Christian theology, whose proponents have often been guilty of excesses in empire-building. There is still a live question, addressed to an extent within this volume, whether therefore all projects of a 'community of communities' are beyond the pale or not – whether there are social goods which should be upheld for all peoples at all times – but it may well be that for Christians this may be as much a time for humility as for forwardness in articulating such a vision in this regard. Perhaps, if history compels us to slow down or, better, refocus our panoramas for the coming of the 'kingdom of God', the major emphasis of the chapters in the pages following is the wise one, namely that communities of belonging and mutual care, wherever they can be sustained and although they cannot make universal claims, are very much in the sphere of interaction with divine purpose and divine belonging.

'Social' theology is focused therefore on the possibilities of human togetherness. It was an obvious comment that the contributors' group was itself engaged if not in perfect social theology then in sociable theology; but, equally obviously, that compels us and our readers to be alert to who was not there. There are many voices unheard in these chapters, whether from particular churches or from constituencies which self-evidently have much to offer in the doing of social theology. We would wish to hear from the visual artists and the philosophers, for example, and from the voices less articulate in the convention of seminar and publication – and most especially, as is noted below, from those who are particularly hurting and forgotten. These chapters only begin to touch on the gifts and promise of, and dangers and troubles and need for, human communities. As a collection, it is only conclusive in affirming that it is right and good to be doing such theology.

Theology

While this collection was put together at the end of a century when so many other social-studies disciplines came newly into their own, it may be wondered whether theology in its own right can be at all contemporary or relevant. Students of theology will be aware how far the discipline of theology has travelled over the centuries and indeed during the course of the twentieth century, to a degree in response to the progress of other academic disciplines. There are indications throughout these chapters of what is a fertile debate on theological method which is conducted both explicitly and implicitly. Given the 'social' qualifier, the intention would be to arrive at, or journey towards, some discernment of the presence of God that can furnish guidance and inspiration for the

making of human community or comunities. As one
respondent put the question in regard to our work in
progress, is it that we aim simply to be kind or to be
faithful? Assuming that the latter is the specifically
Christian option, the work only then begins.
Whether a reader comes to this as a 'non-theologian'
or as someone with theological background and baggage
– and there are combinations, of course, of these two
alternatives! – the lingering question of fundamental
importance is what strength of claim attaches to any
theological conclusions. Biblically, the prophets laid claim
to a direct line to the divine will. If that can be said to
represent the unattainable (certainly as far as the contributors of these chapters are concerned!), the landing-
ground for theological insight will, we hope, still rise
beyond mere human speculation. But it is tentative and
it is both prone to error and capable of refinement. The
group of contributors has been itself strengthened by its
ecumenical and broad composition, but faith and life will
have much more to say than can be expressed in these
pages.

In Scotland Today

With one of the methodological leaps in theology in our
time being the appreciation that all theologies are con-
ditioned – that is, of their time and place – it is however
more than this that is implied in the sub-title, *Doing Social
Theology in Scotland Today*. In different ways, both with
reference to current Scottish experience and personalities
and with the exploration of the Scottish intellectual
tradition, the contributors have attempted to address in
particular the challenges of doing theology in Scotland
around the year 2000. But this is not a confining emphasis,
neither in the sense that outcomes are or will be relevant

only to Scotland (though some particularist insights are
offered) nor in the sense that all that is written here is a
tract for the times, soon to be hopelessly out of date
(though, even as we publish, some issues have moved on).
Again, perhaps the proof of this will lie in the extent to
which we succeed in evoking responses both in and furth
of Scotland, and in time to come! It is incidentally worth
noting that the authors themselves are not all Scotland-
based or (if this matters at all) self-styled Scots. All this
said, it may still be a strange juxtaposition at first sight
for some readers to see 'theology' and 'Scotland today'
in the same sentence; but, for this sort of theological
enterprise, it is an essential crossover.

If it is agreed, then, that doing social theology is a task
for the here and now, there is nevertheless another
important point. It would be all too easy, being so much
concerned with the needs and hopes of our time, to be
blind to horizons not yet glimpsed. The Christian perspective on hope asks that realism, and even more
pessimism, be countered by what may conventionally be
counted even as foolish. Here we come into something
of what it means to have vision – and, although the vision
of what is aimed at may not be clear in all its detail, the
sense that there is a direction to follow and go is the
summons of faith. There is connected with this the
meaning and content of life after death. What can we
hope for? Again and again, the point has to be made that
for truth's sake no lines finally are being drawn on this –
Scotland tomorrow, or the tomorrow of anywhere else
for that matter, will be an issue for tomorrow – but nor
are we forever to be trapped by the mistakes we have
made up to now.

PETER DONALD

Part I

Doing Social Theology: The Scottish Context

A new parliament in Scotland in 1999, with its establishment supported in a popular referendum and therefore taking a share of responsibilities away from Westminster and pursuing constitutionally new ways of working, has had a significant political impact. The time is ripe for asking basic questions, and attempting new answers, concerning the roles and possibilities of governors and governed.

The two opening chapters by Professor Storrar and Dr Blount set out to reflect on the impact of this new political context. In days past, the churches – and in particular the Church of Scotland, the 'Kirk' – would have been in a commanding position to give a lead, in respect both of general cultural trends and of political society. This is no longer the case. Although it is true that in church and state alike there are those who hanker for the ways that (they thought) once were, the times call for new responses and imagination in the framing of any kind of encompassing social vision. A church alliance with power and the established order, qualified in the past by a long history of struggle over issues of sovereignty and therefore church–state relations, is neither appropriate nor sufficient in the present context.

The more traditional issues may continue to surface, but there are newer ones also to be taken into account.

It emerges therefore within these chapters that there are new strategies to be explored, both within the political establishment and within the churches themselves. At both ends, there is a profound need for realism as well as idealism, a self-critical perspective. And beyond what the chapters propound, there are questions which remain to be answered. While so much is to be hoped for through democracy, how are the people to be persuaded to participate? This is not simply a question of apathy, serious though that may be, but also the difficulty of overcoming so long a tradition of exclusion and, in effect, disenfranchisement among various groupings within Scottish society. Second, it has to be asked whether the will of the majority will necessarily set the best paths and what other positions are possible, however unpopular they may be. The point is that diversity, so prominent a feature of contemporary Scottish society, does not easily translate into unity, neither within the churches (alas!) nor certainly more widely. It may be very important to state the goals and to work hard at the means towards their achievement, but there should be no doubting the hugeness of the task of easing tensions for the sake of forging common purpose.

He walks among the yellow and the grey.
Grey of stone and slate and steely rivers
running through grey towns where steel ran yesterday,
and grey mists lifting where the coming day
delivers grey-edged intimations of
a grey mortality and a shadier morality.
Here, poverty and pain are dirty-fingered currency
in the market-place of souls,
and stunted possibility hobbles on the bleeding stumps
of legs hacked off from under it.
Here, in the grey forgotten wasteland
that is not fate of accident or fecklessness
but just the grey, inevitable result
of choices made,
and burdens shifted,
and costs externalised out of the magic circle
of prosperity,
here, he walks.
But in his heart, he carries yellow.
Yellow for the daffodils that surge across the banks of
    railway lines.
Yellow for the crocuses that parade in Charlotte Square.
Yellow for the primroses that glean in crevices of island
    rock.
Yellow for the irises that wave from glittering ditches.
Yellow for the broom that flashed fire across a thousand
    summer hills.

Kathy Galloway, from 'Christ of Scotland'
in Love Burning Deep

I

Democracy and Mission

The New Context for Doing Social Theology

William F. Storrar

What is the new political context for doing Christian social theology in the West at the outset of the twenty-first century? One way of describing this changing context is to speak of a shift from a modern to a post-modern and post-nationalist political world, beyond the contours of the modern nation-state that have dominated the political and constitutional landscape throughout the nineteenth and twentieth centuries. Unlike modern nationalist movements that focused on gaining national independence within a bounded, sovereign state, this new politics can be characterised by a concern for local autonomy within complex and transnational levels of government, with variable and sometimes conflicting jurisdictions within the same territory – the potential demarcation disputes within Scotland, for example, between the Scottish, Westminster and European parliaments, all legislating for and claiming some authority over Scottish affairs. Post-nationalist politics also includes a commitment to active citizenship and participatory democracy, alongside party politics and representative democracy, drawing on the new information technologies and the more benign features of globalisation.

The sociologist David McCrone has argued that
Scotland is a leading example of such post-modern and
post-nationalist political developments.[1] In 1999,
Scotland achieved not modern independence but post-
modern political autonomy. It restored its ancient parliament as a democratic legislature responsible for domestic
affairs, but still within the framework of both the
United Kingdom and the European Union. Scotland now
exists politically within the complex constitutional world
of several levels of legislative, executive and judicial
authority, with variable and continually negotiated jurisdictions and powers.[2] The political movement that
achieved the Scottish parliament in the 1990s was a
cross-party alliance of both home rule (devolutionist and
federalist) and nationalist (pro-independence) parties,
alongside a broad coalition of national institutions and
civic groups from Scottish civil society.[3] Significantly,
the churches and church leaders played a key role in this
movement, alongside trade union and local government
bodies. Another key feature of this coalition was its
strong and self-conscious civic and democratic ethos,
affirming an inclusive and non-ethnic understanding of
Scottish nationhood and identity. In a referendum on
setting up the Scottish parliament held in 1997, a
legislative body on Scottish affairs with limited fiscal
powers was endorsed by a convincing majority vote on
an impressive electoral turnout. At the turn of the
millennium, here was an example of a peaceful and
inclusive national movement for constitutional change
that was successful through active citizenship and for
democratic not ethnic ends.

Given similar movements across the West and around
the world – alongside and never forgetting continuing
ethnic conflicts and worsening problems of poverty,
predatory globalisation and environmental degradation

– what can be learned from the Scottish experience of
this emerging new politics? In Scotland, as elsewhere,
democratic renewal is clearly rooted in an active and
autonomous local civil society, connecting with a wider
global civil society, rather than set within the 'modern'
world of self-contained nation-states. How should
Christian social theology interact with this very particular political and cultural development; and what
insights, if any, does such a public theology have to offer
concerned members of both church and society?

I wish to frame my own tentative theological responses
to this emerging new local and global political context
within the wider horizon of mission. Why relate democracy primarily to mission, rather than more obviously
to a Christian concern with public justice, for example?
I would give two reasons for making what I regard to be
the crucial linkage for doing social theology in the post-
modern political context of the twenty-first century,
linking democracy and mission. The first reason for
linking democracy and mission stems from a small but
significant theological blind spot in Scotland in the late
1960s, and the second reason stems from a large and
seminal theological vision of the nature of mission
emerging from South Africa in the early 1990s.

During the first post-war surge in electoral support
for Scottish nationalism in the late 1960s, the then
Labour government set up an independent Royal Commission on the Constitution that took evidence from
various public bodies, including the Church of Scotland,
a long-term supporter of devolution. During questioning
by Commission members on the reasons for the Church
of Scotland's support for Scottish self-government, the
church spokesperson claimed that this support was based
on the national church's role as a representative national
institution, 'widely representative of public opinion in

Scotland'. When asked how a new political context after Scottish self-government might strengthen the church's witness to the Gospel, the church spokesperson replied: 'I do not think that this is an element which has entered into our calculations at all.' This answer was meant to indicate an honourable lack of institutional self-interest on the church's part. However, it surely also betrays a more serious lack of theological understanding of the nature of mission and its essential relationship to the contemporary political context. It is telling that it was the Commission member who was astute enough to respond with the comment: 'I do not think that I have had an answer [to my question].' Whether that Commission member realised it or not, he was asking a profound theological and missiological question that the church could not answer – was there a connection between the church's support for political change and its witness to the Gospel? This is a question at the very core of the church's identity and purpose. In the late 1960s, the Church of Scotland could not even see the question clearly, never mind give an adequate answer.

I have argued elsewhere that one of the main reasons why the Church of Scotland's public voice fell silent in the first and failed referendum on Scottish self-government in 1979 was because it was based on this inherited identity and assumed authority as a national institution representative of public opinion.[4] When public support for devolution fell away in 1979, the ground on which the church had chosen to make its stand also shook and left it wrong-footed and unsure of its position. The Church of Scotland in the late 1980s learned from this earlier failure, and based its continuing support for constitutional change and democratic renewal in the 1990s on explicitly theological grounds, centred on its public witness to the Gospel and its own radical

Reformed tradition of reflection on the nature and limits of state power (Church and Nation Report, 1989). Paradoxically, when the Church of Scotland was still in a position of relative institutional and numerical strength as a national church in the 1960s, it chose to speak out of the strength of that identity as a national institution on a major public issue but brought no socially significant influence to bear on the outcome of events in 1979. Yet in the 1990s, when the Church of Scotland was in serious numerical decline as a national church, with a steeply falling membership, it chose to speak out of its witness to the Gospel and was perceived, in partnership with its fellow churches and civic bodies, to have played a small but significant role in the broad civic and cross-party movement that achieved a decisive victory in the 1997 referendum on the establishment of a Scottish parliament – not least for making a Reformed and ecumenical theological case for the limited sovereignty of the people under God, as opposed to the prevailing constitutional doctrine of the unlimited sovereignty of the Westminster parliament.[5]

This Scottish experience shows that where the churches make the connection between their public engagement and their witness to the Gospel – in an understanding of mission that includes both a critical affirmation of the political dimension of life and a healthy suspicion of any final and unexamined identification of the Gospel with any particular cause – then an authentic Christian social theology can flourish even in the midst of the institutional shaking and shrinking of the mainstream, established churches.

The second, compelling reason to link democracy and mission in any development of an adequate social theology today stems from the work of that remarkable and deeply missed South African mission thinker, the late David Bosch. He set out his persuasive and magisterial argument for an emerging, ecumenical and postmodern paradigm of mission in his seminal and now classic work, *Transforming Mission*.[6] As Bosch wrote of what he regarded as one key strand in this new paradigm, the liberation theology arising out of Latin America: 'It is not a fad but a serious attempt to let the faith make sense to the postmodern age.'[7]

Bosch showed that the struggle for justice and liberation from oppression that we witnessed in his native South Africa in the 1990s is as much a dimension of God's mission to the world in Jesus Christ as the invitation to personal discipleship in evangelism or the call to pastoral care of the vulnerable and needy in works of compassion. What Bosch argued for, and traced in the thinking of different Christian traditions in the later twentieth century, was the convergence of these two essential elements, the political and the pastoral, in the emerging ecumenical understanding of mission. Here, mission is fundamentally not what the church does in missions but what God is doing in the world as creator, redeemer and giver of life. God's mission, the *missio Dei*, is the dynamic mission of this trinitarian God in the midst of life and on the dusty road. It is when we set our commitment to more just and participatory political, economic and social structures within this emerging new paradigm of mission which Bosch left as his lasting legacy that we find the spiritual and theological resources to sustain the Christian hope in the midst of suffering, failure and our painful longing for the Kingdom that is not yet. Fellow South African theologians and witnesses like Desmond Tutu, John de Gruchy, Charles Villa-Vicencio, Piet Meiring and many others have carried forward this vision of David Bosch in thought and practice, linking democracy and mission in the develop-

ment of relevant social theologies for the new South
Africa – not least in the powerful linking of justice and
mercy in the extraordinary work of the Truth and
Reconciliation Commission.[8] Those of us who would
develop social theologies in our own emerging post-
modern political contexts need to see at the heart of
South Africa's witness to the Gospel this not uncritical
linking of the frail search for flawed democracy and
the continual seeking after the integrity of authentic
Christian mission.

Such theological reflection on the churches' experience of political involvement in both Scotland and
South Africa affirms this evangelical connection between
democracy and mission – the biblical connection between
justice, mercy and the knowledge of God. What insights
can we gain from such experiences in the late twentieth
century about the nature of the new post-modern
political context in the twenty-first century, with its
search for post-nationalist autonomy and an active
and empowered citizenship within a flourishing local
and global civil society? I think that what we can see
emerging is exactly what David Bosch prepared us to
expect, *a new convergence of the pastoral and the
political in the twenty-first century*. It is certainly what
I think we can see emerging in our own particular
Scottish experience of this much wider, global phenomenon. But, to see that convergence, we need to enjoy
God's joke on post-modern Scots, and then, perhaps, on
the rest of us.

Holyrood: A *Holy* Parliament

Sometimes, to describe something in a more telling way,
we are driven to comic juxtapositions: the combination
of two unlikely, seemingly contradictory terms in the

same descriptive phrase. So, we might speak of sun-drenched Scotland! Yahweh, the God of the Hebrew Bible, seems particularly fond of such jokes. This God calls Israel a *holy* nation. Given that the term *nation* in the Old Testament is synonymous with the wickedness and idolatry of the Gentile world, to be called a *holy nation* is akin to being called an incorruptible mafia. In the New Testament, the church is also called a holy nation. Given the history of the Christian church, in all its folly and cruelty since Constantine, God's joke is on us as well.

Like all good jokes, it is rooted in a profound theological truth. As we are reminded in the season of Lent, God the tragi-comedian chooses the crooks of this world to make known God's holy love for the world: the deceiving supplanter Jacob who became faithful Israel; the convicted thief who was pardoned by the divine love at his side, on Calvary. The profoundest joke of all is to speak of the *holy* Cross – that 'healthy killing machine', where the fateful tragedy of death and despair becomes the unexpected comic ending of resurrection and hope.

I could not help but think of this divine tragi-comedy when, in the inscrutable wisdom of the Scottish Office, the then Secretary of State for Scotland, Donald Dewar, announced the site of the new Scottish parliament in Edinburgh – Holyrood, the place of the Holy Rood, Christ's Cross. Not for Dewar the expected site on Calton Hill, with its classical Royal High School, a building redolent of ancient Greek democracy and Roman gravitas. No, the new parliament was to be built on a comic site *par excellence*, the former site of a brewery bearing the name of a gallows.

Once again, the joke is on us – Holyrood, a *holy* parliament! Given the low esteem in which politicians and parliaments are held around the world, we should savour this comic juxtaposition. And yet, in the mystery of the divine love, if not by political design, it is an appropriate name for the new parliament.

The place of Christ's Rood, his Cross, is the place where we see shockingly juxtaposed God's suffering love for humanity with the terminal violence of the powerful against the innocent. It is a *holy* place precisely because it is a place of healing for a suffering world. Through the resurrection and the sending of the Spirit, the holy rood remains a source of hope for humanity. I wish to suggest that the theological significance of the new structures and processes of the Scottish parliament lies in their capacity to bring something of that cruciform holiness to our politics, to our people, and to our small bit of the planet.

Now, to make a call for holiness on the eve of the new Scottish parliament is a dumb move. The word *holy* has rightly had a bad odour in Scotland. We all think of the poet Robert Burns's *Holy Willie*, a brilliant and withering satire on Calvinist religious and moral hypocrisy. We think with shame of religious wars, spewing lethal hatreds and daring to do so in the name of Christ. In thinking of Holyrood as the *holy* parliament, I am not suggesting that the goal of the churches is to turn the Scottish parliament into a moralising arena for political holy Willies or a new theocracy to oppress non-Christians or non-believers – God forbid. No, I am suggesting that the churches at least take seriously the tragi-comic symbolism of the parliament's name, Holyrood, and seek to make it a holy place for all those living in Scotland and for all parts of Scotland.

The word *holy* in the Bible means that which is set apart for God. Here, I have in mind not so much that biblical notion of set-apartness but the association in the English language between words for holiness and wholeness. The root of the English word *holy* is the Old English word *halig*, literally meaning *whole*. Our English word *holy* is therefore connected with the idea of being whole; that is, according to Chambers' Dictionary, being *sound in health, uninjured, restored to health, healed, not broken, undamaged, not broken up or ground, or deprived of any part*. When we combine these root meanings of holiness as wholeness and health in Old English with the New Testament equation of health with salvation – and the Cross as their paradoxical source – then we can see the Holy Rood with a fresh eye, as the place of wholeness and healing for an unhealthy, injured, broken, damaged, ground-down and deprived world. This wholeness and healing are only possible, of course, because of Jesus, the holy one of Israel, set apart and anointed for God's saving purposes in the world. As the one who is fully human and yet without sin, Jesus died in our place as broken sinners and for a broken world, in that wonderful exchange of death for life on the Cross, the place of the Holy Rood. It is the Risen Christ's death on the Holy Rood and life-giving gift of the Holy Spirit that makes possible the dynamic of personal, social and cosmic healing and wholeness associated with the Old English word *halig*.

Indeed, in the New Testament, holiness as set-apartness is also understood in this same dynamic way. The *holy* refers not to sacred places or objects or rituals but to the life-giving movement of the *Holy* Spirit in the world; the Spirit who is the gift of the new age inaugurated by Jesus in his own person and rule. To speak of the holy is therefore to discern the signs of life brought by the Spirit.[9] As the German theologian Jürgen Moltmann has put it:

Jesus did not bring a new religion into the world. He brought new life . . . He brought life into this dying and violent world . . . Christ is the divine Yes to life. That Yes leads to the healing of the sick, to the acceptance of the marginalized, to the forgiveness of sins, and to the saving of impaired lives from the power of destruction. This is the way the Gospels tell of Jesus' mission. And according to the Gospels this is also the character of the mission of the women and the men who live in his Spirit. (Matthew 10:7–8)[10]

It is in this sense that I wish to speak of Holyrood as the holy parliament. Parliaments are not divine saviours but frail human institutions coping with conflicting demands, unyielding limits and the unrelenting temptations of power. To call a parliament holy is a comic juxtaposition, like holy nation or holy cross. Yet it reminds us that even Holyrood in all its frailty could be and should be a life-giving place working for the holiness of Scotland. By holiness, I do not mean any return to a puritan past or a Christian nation. I hope it is clear by now that I mean the full-bodied wholeness and the creative life we should think of when we draw on the semantic well of that Old English word *halig* and the divine well of the *Holy* Spirit.

A strong objection can be made to the argument so far, that the theological significance of the parliament lies in its potential for creating wholeness and healing: that what Holyrood requires from the churches is a pastoral theology of power and a holiness theology of politics. Is this not all New Age platitude? What the parliament needs from the churches is the courageous prophetic voice, condemning the pride and arrogance of our new rulers and calling the powerful relentlessly to justice – a Nathan denouncing David, a Bonhoeffer denouncing Hitler, a Tutu confronting de Klerk – not this soft talk about holiness as wholeness and health.

Yes, the prophetic is one way of providing a theological interpretation of the new parliament, and it has its proper place. The church must never shrink from its biblical calling to name and condemn sin in those people, structures and systems wielding power in the state and public life. Perhaps the outstanding examples of that in the twentieth century in the West are in the Confessing Church's Barmen Declaration in 1934 in Germany against the Nazis, the South African churches' Kairos Declaration for a prophetic stance against apartheid, and the critique of the inherent sinfulness of groups and nations, made so effectively by the American theologian Reinhold Niebuhr. There is a time and a place for the churches' prophetic voice. But is there also a time and a place in post-modern politics for another pastoral voice? Or is a pastoral approach to the political a dereliction of prophetic duty?

A Pastoral Approach to Politics

Let me respond to this criticism of a pastoral understanding of politics – as the pursuit of holiness as wholeness – with three counter-criticisms from the perspective of a pastoral theology of power. First, as the feminist theologian Daphne Hampson has reminded us, Reinhold Niebuhr's widely influential discussion of sin in politics is gender-biased. Sin as pride may be appropriate to men, calling for prophetic denunciation. But, for the majority of the population, women, she argues that the problem is one not of self-assertion but of the lack of self-actualisation in the midst of so many demands at home, in the family and at work. So Hampson observes:

> Much theology has indeed been written by men divorced from the daily round of chores, from the human lifecycle

of caring and nurturing; theology has been a preoccupation of monks, bishops and professors. No wonder that the human being whom they take as the norm is the isolated male.[11]

An appropriate theological interpretation of the new political structures and processes must take Hampson's criticism into account. One of the most politically significant developments accompanying the Scottish parliament is the commitment to gender equality among elected representatives and to family-friendly hours and facilities for MSPs and their children. Along with that is the commitment to the equality agenda in all legislation, 'to promote equal opportunities for women, people with disabilities, ethnic minorities and other groups'.[12] We need to assess the parliament theologically and practically in terms of its promotion of human self-actualisation for women, minorities and the disabled; a complex and slow business for the churches compared with the prophet's denunciations of those proud politicians.

This leads me on to my second comment, which arises out of my own pastoral experience in the 1980s. As a minister and pastor, I once had to accompany an elderly parent to the Sheriff Court to seek a legal order to take a mentally ill family member into hospital, on medical advice. The strain caused the elderly parent to collapse and the sheriff to clear the court. As I waited in the corridor, the consultant psychiatrist giving evidence turned angrily to me and said that this person's collapse was caused directly by the government's change in the mental-health legislation for Scotland, requiring us to go through the courts. Westminster had brought us into line with England to tackle problems in the English mental-health system which we never had in Scotland in the first place. My pastoral experience in this and in too many cases was that inappropriate legislation or state action could literally be lethal, destroying health and lives among the most vulnerable in our community: the unemployed, the frail elderly, the handicapped, those subject to abuse and domestic violence, and the mentally ill. As all legislation at Holyrood is to be audited in this way, to test its outcomes on its impact on the most vulnerable, we need a critical and not a soft theology of wholeness and health to evaluate this new type of legislative process.

That brings me on to my final point in reply to any cynicism about a theology of holiness for Holyrood. In 1999, the British Prime Minister Tony Blair made a commitment 'to lift . . . 60,000 children in Scotland out of poverty by the end of this Parliament' (*The Scotsman*, 19 March 1999). This policy commitment is both commendable and shameful. It exposes yet again the terrible scale and the awful reality of poverty in Scotland, especially among children, where their life-expectancy, general health, educational attainments and employment opportunities are already fixed at birth as significantly less than those of children living in more affluent neighbouring areas. This is the Scotland for which Holyrood has taken responsibility in the twenty-first century. If the churches are not talking the holiness agenda of wholeness and health for children – the biblical litmus test of justice, mercy and the knowledge of God – with the parliament on a daily basis, then we will have failed utterly to see and practise the liberating theological significance of the place of the Holy Rood.

One appropriate way, then, of offering a theological interpretation and critique of the new Scottish parliament's work is to consider the potential of its new structures and processes for bringing some more substantial measure of wholeness and healing to the most vulnerable in Scotland. As in any post-modern context, the pastoral is the political. In order to make this holiness agenda more concrete, I want now to consider briefly three aspects of post-modern civic democracy – *the parliament's structures, processes and outcomes*. In what ways, then, can we expect these new parliamentary structures, democratic processes and policy outcomes to be the work of a *holy* parliament, a parliament making for wholeness and life in Scotland?

Locating the Parliament's Political Structures

First, the parliament's political structures. To make Holyrood work, to make for a holy parliament, we cannot leave the new politics to the parties and the elected politicians. We need to locate the parliament's new democratic structures within the wider political context of a healthy culture of active citizenship in Scottish civil society. As Stephen Maxwell has commented, on the role of that civil society in relation to the new parliament:

> If the Members of the Scottish Parliament remain true to their parties' promises and the expectations of the Scottish public, the Scottish Parliament by contrast [with Westminster] will engage Scottish society in an active and wide-ranging collaboration in legislation and in scrutinising the executive. This commitment to engage with wider Scottish society comes . . . from a changed understanding of the requirements of effective government. In a complex modern society the state cannot govern by legislative fiat. It needs to inform and improve its policies by tapping the expertise and experience of society as a whole. And to implement its policies it needs to mobilise the support of organised social interests and groups outwith the state. These interests and groups make up civil society.[13]

In other words, Holyrood and its fairly elected, gender-balanced MSPs are not enough to ensure the holiness of Scotland. The wholeness and health of Scottish society are as much dependent on an active civil society as they are on the activities of the new Scottish parliament. As Maxwell recognises, the churches are an important part of Scottish civil society and they have a significant role to play in the new politics.

One way in which that civil society is now finding its voice in Scottish public affairs is through the recently founded national Civic Forum, in which most of the mainstream Scottish churches are members through the ecumenical body ACTS. This new Civic Forum is funded by the Scottish government as an important component in the new democratic settlement in Scotland. I would go further and argue that the flourishing of the new Civic Forum, and the varied and complex sectors and organisations of civil society which it represents, is fundamental and essential to the flourishing of democracy and good government at Holyrood. Therefore, the churches should have a particular concern for strengthening the fabric of civil society and the influence and standing of the Civic Forum, as perhaps their best way of looking after the democratic well-being of the Scottish parliament itself.

We cannot begin to locate the structures of the parliament within the purposes of God for human and environmental flourishing in Scotland unless we locate them in the related flourishing of civil society. Such a pastoral theological interpretation of the civic conditions for Holyrood's own political health requires the churches to make a paradigm shift in their own thinking about politics in Scotland. We not only need to locate the parliament within the life-giving environment of an active civil society; we also need to relocate the churches' theological thinking and public pronouncements about that parliament in the twenty-first century and not leave them stranded in the eighteenth century.

When the old Scottish parliament was adjourned in May 1707, Scotland was still in the world of Christendom, where church–state relations were central to the churches' political concerns and goal of preserving a Christian society. Now, in the opening years of the twenty-first century, and with a new Scottish parliament, the social, religious and political world of Christendom has all but gone, and a new pluralist and participatory society is upon us in Scotland. We live in post-modern times, when church–citizen relations in civil society are proving more important for the churches' goals than any formal relationship with the state, even the Scottish parliament. This requires the churches to develop a new theology of citizenship for a pluralist society and participatory democracy, rather than vainly trying to hold on to the remnants of their old power as the church establishment in a Unionist Britain, or even trying to seize denominational hegemony in an independent Scotland.

As Duncan Forrester has reminded us, 'with the recognition that Christendom has passed away beyond recall, there remains an urgent need for a post-Christendom political theology . . . not wistful but forward-looking and missionary, taking the political realm with profound seriousness, but never making it absolute'.[14] A holy parliament at Holyrood in the twenty-first century, whole and healthy in the exercise of its proper powers and responsibilities, will require the churches to develop such a missionary approach to the structures of power; not wistful for the old top-down cosiness of church–state relations in the pre-modern era or romanticising its revolutionary role as a base-up leader of the masses, as in the modern era, but humbly accepting its role as a social partner in the side-by-side culture of post-modernity. The Scottish churches need to be forward-looking, taking the emerging civic realm with profound seriousness without making its own institutional self-interest in relation to the state absolute. As I have argued, this missionary concern leads me on to the second aspect of our theological scrutiny of Holyrood, the need to evangelise the parliament's new democratic processes.

Evangelising the Parliament's Democratic Processes

What kind of missionary political theology do the churches need to engage with the new political order? Well, the democratic processes proposed for Holyrood are impressive in the range of possibilities for participation and influence that they offer not only to backbench MSPs but also to citizens and civic bodies. Andrew Burns has identified five operating principles undergirding the new decision-making and legislative processes in the new parliament: accountability to the electorate through more democratic structures; transparency of policy-making through the parliament's openness and access to public and civic bodies; distribution of power to a strong parliamentary committee structure with powers to initiate as well as scrutinise legislation; elected representatives who reflect the diversity of the Scottish population and nationwide interests; and a commitment to working through consensus and co-operation.[15]

The question is, how can we make these admirable principles operational in the actual decision-making processes of the Scottish parliament? For the churches, this means: how can we evangelise these processes with those attitudes and practices which reflect the Gospel's commitment to Kingdom values? Such Kingdom values are not identical with Holyrood's five principles, but they are sympathetic to them and supportive of them. Those principles are highly vulnerable to the inevitable political undertow of government secrecy, party conflict, competing special interests and electoral popularity. To survive and flourish in this harsh political atmosphere, the democratic processes will need from the churches a realist doctrine of those ambiguities and entrenched patterns of human sin which make all human endeavours for accountability, openness and cooperation too difficult to maintain.

There are two ways in which the churches can help sustain a favourable climate here. The first is to insist that decision-making in the new parliament is a moral and spiritual matter and not just a technical or ideological debate about the allocation of scarce resources or party preferences. This was brought home to me in the 1997 referendum campaign on a Scottish parliament. During that campaign, the civic group *Common Cause* organised civic forums on the referendum's implications for Scotland's future, including one in Inverness. There, as the journalist and writer Neal Ascherson, one of the forum speakers, records:

> An old man in the town house in Inverness said, 'Never again will this chance come. Your fathers and grandfathers look down on you', and I heard a hiss of indrawn breath all round me. 'Let politics look after itself – this is a moral and a spiritual decision', and the sober citizenry broke into applause.[16]

Of course, the old man was right: the referendum was a unique chance which the nation seized with every ballot box. If the Scottish people had not taken it, then the parliament would never have come in our lifetime. But given that we did realise that possibility of change, the truth is that the chance to change Scotland's future now comes every day, in every decision of the Scottish parliament. And every decision will be a moral and spiritual choice – will the MSPs and civil servants, the interest groups and parties, the civic bodies and citizens, make each decision according to the five principles of the new democracy, or will they revert to the old politics? Reverting to old ways is a real possibility, judging by both political experience over centuries and moral experience over millennia. The call to prophetic protest in the millennium may well be about protecting the fragile fabric and networks of public participation against old political moths; less about dramatic public confrontation with tyrants and more about patient endurance in nurturing the life-cycle of open government.

But the churches must also equip their members to be active in that moral and spiritual battle for the health and wholeness of the new democratic processes. So, secondly, the churches must practise similar ways of working in their own internal life and politics, as working models of open government to educate their members into the ethos and mores of active citizenship and participatory democracy in the wider society. The churches need to evangelise their own institutions, to be converted themselves to new ways of open decision-making, power-sharing, collaborative leadership and accountability, especially involving women, the young and their own poorer or disabled members, if they are to equip their lay members to be evangelists for democratic conversion and ecologists for a participatory environment in the new political system. Both are Gospel matters.

Auditing the Parliament's Policy Outcomes

Finally, a pastoral theological vision of a holy parliament, working for the wholeness and healing of the nation – its environment, its poor and marginal, its citizens at large – must give equal attention to Holyrood's policy outcomes, as well as the location and operation of its democratic structures and policy-making processes. Keith Clements, in his book *Learning to Speak: The Church's Voice in Public Affairs*, has argued that the churches need to recover the role of the learner in public affairs, before they are ready to speak out.[17] I would go further. The churches after Christendom also need to find a role and discipline as listeners, learning to listen to the cries of the people in their midst.

There is an emerging consensus that the Holyrood parliament should audit its policies as to their likely effect on the lives of the poor and on the environment. One of the best ways in which the churches can complement that process is through listening to the impact of these audited policies on the lives of the communities and places in which they live and serve. To be an auditor is to be a hearer. The churches and their clergy are one of the last national bodies to retain a residential presence in every community in Scotland, including the more deprived urban and rural areas. Out of that ubiquitous presence, the churches are almost uniquely placed to give voice to what they hear from their neighbours, the length and breadth of Scotland, and from around the world. The God of the Bible is the God who hears the cries of the slaves in Egypt and the groans of a creation in bondage to decay and the yearnings of the troubled human heart, too deep for words. The Spirit helps us to give audible voice to these laboured sounds. As communities of faith open to the Spirit, the churches must also learn to listen to these sounds of oppression, despoliation and despair, under the impact of Holyrood's policies and laws or from any other source, local or global – and then to help articulate them to those in power, in partnership with their neighbours. One of the surest signs of health and wholeness, one of the surest signs of the life-giving Spirit, is when we hear the cries of our neighbour. To paraphrase the parable, 'for I was silenced and you heard me' is surely the Lord's Word to post-modern democracies.

Conclusion: Leaves from the Scottish Parliament

In 1999, there was a public exhibition in Edinburgh on the Darien Scheme, that tragi-comic failed attempt by the Scots to set up a trading colony in Panama in the 1690s. Documents on display told the story of this ill-fated Scottish attempt at imperialism under its own blue banner (they showed a greater eye for self-advancement under the later British imperial banner). Of particular interest is the record of the Scottish parliament on display, minuting the parliament's business on the day that it considered the legislation on Darien, setting up the national trading company in which much of Scotland's wealth was invested. The day began, as all days began in the old Scottish parliament, with prayers.

In other words, there were prayers on the day on which the old Scottish parliament sent this nation on course for virtual bankruptcy, leading on to the weak Scottish negotiating position with England that led in turn to an incorporating rather than a federal parliamentary union, a folly that has taken us almost 300 years to mend. There were prayers in the parliament on the day it sent the Darien settlers on their way to ruin and death, and subjected the indigenous peoples of that isthmus to yet another round of European colonial conquest, rivalry and violence. Cast your eye across the same page of the parliamentary record on the Darien Scheme and you will see the minute on the enquiry into the Glencoe massacre, a Scottish domestic act of official violence and cover-up. Business on that day began with prayer as well.

It is a sober reminder of the real theological issue at stake in the structures and processes, the procedures and outcomes of the new Scottish parliament. Prayers in parliament are a necessary but not a sufficient condition of bearing witness to God's reign in public life. The Holyrood parliament also begins its weekly legislative plenary session with a suitably post-modern form of prayer, a time for reflection taken by a range of believers, through different faiths and humanisms. The content of each Time for Reflection is entered into the leaves of the official parliamentary record. But the parliamentary minutes recording Holyrood's business will be judged ultimately on the health and life, or the sickness and death, that the prayerful actions of the Scottish parliament brought to the nation, and to the wide earth. The Holyrood parliament is the site of great hopes and expectations for the people of Scotland and for friends of democracy around the world. Whether its leaves of record will fall like the leaves on the Tree of Life in Revelation, for the healing of the nations, remains to be seen. But, even if the business of Holyrood turns at times into a record of farce or tragedy, we cannot but believe that the God of the Holy Rood will have the last holy, healing laugh.

That was certainly my prayer when I conducted the Time for Reflection in the Scottish parliament in June 2001. I suggested that, when the MSPs move from their temporary home on the Mound to the permanent

Holyrood parliament building at the foot of the Royal Mile, and enter the new legislative chamber for the very first session, they should take off their shoes, for they will be walking on holy ground, the place where laws are made and lives are changed, for good or ill: the place of the Holy Rood.

Notes

1. David McCrone, *Understanding Scotland: The Sociology of a Nation*, 2nd edn, London: Routledge, 2001.
2. Neil MacCormick, *Questioning Sovereignty*, Oxford: Oxford University Press, 1999, esp. ch. 7.
3. Christopher Harvie and Peter Jones, *The Road to Home Rule*, Edinburgh: Polygon, 2000.
4. William F. Storrar, *Scottish Identity: A Christian Vision*, Edinburgh: Handsel Press, 1990, pp. 202–11.
5. Peter Lynch, *Scottish Government and Politics*, Edinburgh: Edinburgh University Press, 2000.
6. David Bosch, *Transforming Mission*, Maryknoll, NY: Orbis, 1991.
7. Ibid., p. 447.
8. Piet Meiring, *Chronicle of the Truth Commission*, Vanderbijlpark, South Africa: Carpe Diem Books, 1999.
9. Colin Brown, general ed., *Dictionary of New Testament Theology*, Vol. 2, Grand Rapids, Michigan: Zondervan, 1967, pp. 223–38.
10. Jürgen Moltmann, *God for a Secular Society*, London: SCM Press, 1999, p. 241.
11. Daphne Hampson, 'Reinhold Niebuhr on sin: a critique', in Richard Harries, ed., *Reinhold Niebuhr and the Issues of our Time*, Oxford: Mowbray, 1986, pp. 51–2.
12. Gerry Hassan and Chris Warhurst, *The New Scottish Politics*, Norwich: The Stationery Office, 2000, p. 139.
13. Ibid., p. 133.
14. Duncan B. Forrester, *Theology and Politics*, Oxford: Basil Blackwell, 1988, p. 55.
15. Hassan and Warhurst, eds, *The New Scottish Politics*, pp. 52, 53.

16. Neal Ascherson, 'Some poetry, pipers and politics for the people', in Lindsay Paterson, ed., *A Diverse Assembly: The Debate on the Scottish Parliament*, Edinburgh: Edinburgh University Press, 1998, pp. 306–7.

17. Keith Clements, *Learning to Speak: The Church's Voice in Public Affairs*, Edinburgh: T&T Clark, 1995.

Atween the world o' licht
And the world that is to be
A man wi' unco sicht
Sees where he canna see:

Gangs whaur he canna walk
Recks whaur he canna read
Hauds what he canna tak
Mells wi' the unborn dead.

William Soutar (1898–1943)
from *Scotland*

2

A New Voice in a New Land?

Graham K. Blount

Despite the imposing statue of John Knox on its doorstep, the Scottish parliament has been born into a world quite different from that in which Knox and Mary Queen of Scots competed for authority. Marking its first 1,000 days, the parliament made a movie, or at least a short film, as 'a modest tribute to all the people who have already spoken to parliament'; its title echoed Donald Dewar's words at the opening – 'there is a new voice in the land, the voice of a democratic parliament'. The accompanying press release also noted, rather defensively, that parliament had enacted thirty bills, held over 1,200 committee meetings (twenty-eight of them outside Edinburgh), received 480 petitions and dealt with over 24,000 written parliamentary questions.

The defensiveness about what has been achieved reacts to a tide of media-led cynicism, but the decision to focus on those who have spoken *to* (rather than *in* or *for*) parliament is also significant. For some, the defining moment of parliament's first year was the expert evidence brought by Lothian Anti-Poverty Alliance to the then Social Inclusion Committee, in which two people told their own stories of what debt, and debt-recovery methods, had meant to them. Alongside all the other relevant expertise, that evidence changed the minds of MSPs, and committed them to supporting the bill to abolish warrant sales, despite pressure from the Executive. That victory in principle remains incomplete, as the Executive succeeded in delaying implementation and introduced an alternative that some fear may not be radically different from the warrant sales which had been abolished. But there was in this a vindication of several aspects of the new democratic process:

- *Access*, in the sense of all kinds of people being able to air their grievances and contribute their experience and expertise – as sheriff officers or debtors – to the decision-making process;

- *Fairness*, in an electoral system which, through proportional representation, produced a Scottish Socialist Party MSP who would not have been elected under a first-past-the-post system, and gave that MSP the power (with enough support but without the need to win a back-bench ballot as at Westminster) to initiate a bill and have it mean-ingfully debated;

- *Sharing of power*, through a system that gives genuine power to committees involving all the four main parties, which can build their own con-sensus even in opposition to the Executive.

Although there are disturbing signs that the 'growing up' process of the parliament may undermine these aspirations, this is still no one person's parliament, nor one political party's. Donald Dewar's determination that 'there shall be a Scottish parliament' delivered what had not only been the hope of many (including the Scottish churches) but had also been shaped co-operatively by politicians and people through the Constitutional

Convention (again, conspicuously, including the churches). Recognition of the importance of New Labour's delivery of the parliament, as part of its strategy for modernising government, should not undermine the narrative which sees the Scottish parliament as not so much a creature 'ex nihilo', *established* by the modernisers of the Blair government in Westminster, as a body giving legislative form to what was *claimed* as the settled will of the Scottish people, *confirmed* by referendum and *recognised* by the UK parliament.

Perhaps the most crucial contribution the Kirk made to the movement that gave birth to the parliament was a theological one, locating the devolution debate in the context of an understanding of sovereignty. In this traditional Scots understanding, which starts from the sovereignty of God, divine sovereignty is seen as entrusted to the 'community of the realm' (citizens of Scotland), who may then trust the administration of their affairs, from time to time, to a variety of individuals or institutions. This understanding, which underpinned the 'Claim of Right' and the Constitutional Convention, seems far more appropriate to the complexities of power and authority in the globalised world than the inflexible Westminster doctrine of the sovereignty of the Crown in parliament. In that sense, it remains our parliament under God, with as inclusive a sense of ownership as can be achieved; its founding principles of power-sharing, access, accountability, participation and equal opportunities were the framework set out by the Consultative Steering Group to secure that. Churches, then, remain stakeholders – perhaps even godparents – in the parliament.

Of course, the reality has sometimes been frustratingly less than that, and a reluctance to go its own way against London's lead. When the Scottish parliament appeared to take a distinctive line on care for the elderly, immediate reactions from Westminster suggested that the reality of devolution had still to dawn; some Scottish Labour MPs seemed to assume that party discipline would achieve the harmonisation of policy that the Westminster parliament could no longer impose. Yet that commitment to free personal care for the elderly was the key achievement celebrated by the Executive as marking the parliament's third birthday.

The most public defining issue for parliament's first year was the acrimonious debate over 'Clause 28/2a', throughout which there was, in and beyond the churches, a deep sense of grievance that 'the parliament wasn't listening' to the views of what seemed to be the clear majority of Scots. The model of 'consultation' here, in which a clear policy pronouncement is made at the outset by the Executive, is almost inevitably going to seem unreal; and the often vicious and personalised sloganising across billboards and tabloid headlines was far from constructive engagement between parliament and people. However, the process did eventually stumble towards a kind of compromise (if not consensus) that addressed some of the concerns raised by those opposed to repeal.

In the longer term, what does this episode mean for the churches' engagement with the parliament, and what does it say for the media's relationship to parliament? The negative attitude of most of Scotland's press to the parliament whose creation they generally supported has taken people by surprise. In particular, the hostility of the traditionally Labour-supporting *Daily Record*, vividly but not exclusively illustrated over Clause 2a, took the Labour Party aback; and the stance of Andrew Neil's *Scotsman* bemused much of its core readership. Perhaps the Scottish media reacted against an expectation that they would be parliament's cheerleaders, or perhaps sniping from the sidelines represented the easier option. In the longer term, what is worrying is the extent to which their treatment of the parliament has limited the possibilities of 'new politics'. It is the confrontational politics of a 'question time' increasingly pushed into a Westminster model that is deemed exciting enough to report, while consensus emerging from hard work and genuine listening in Committees is seen as dull.

There is good journalism about (in tabloids and broadsheets), and an effective *Daily Record* campaign against loan sharks recently sparked parliamentary debate on the spiral of poverty and debt; but the prevailing media culture cheapens politics and politicians in public perception, and also pushes the politicians into fitting the media profile in order to gain the 'oxygen of publicity'. It would be a mistake to underestimate how much political behaviour is motivated by defensiveness against 'what the papers (might) say'.

Much of what has been called the 'pious vocabulary' of the parliament has been aspirational rather than consistently carried through. Initial resistance to the 'yah-boo' of Westminster is waning and seems unlikely to survive the temptations of a predetermined election dominating the horizon for parliament's fourth year. Committees (now generally applauded in the media as the best thing about the new politics, but still rarely reported by them) are rearranged at the behest of party managers, undermining the build-up of consensus, expertise and identity, and moving some of those back-benchers not quite on-message into areas where they might have less prominence. Coalition or partnership politics comes under increasing pressure to put party discipline at its core. Committees increasingly meet in private, without serious criticism from media who (in a highly competitive business) prioritise securing 'exclusive' leaks over opening up parliament to public scrutiny.

Our theology might lead us not only to expect the (sinful?) old to reassert itself in the midst of the new, but also to reflect that 'pious vocabulary' needs a constant reality-check to prevent its deterioration into shibboleths.

If the debate over sex education has, for some in the churches and among politicians, been seen as defining relations between churches and parliament, this may be in terms of churches defending a corner fairly narrowly defined in terms of 'traditional moral values', against a parliament perceived as pushing a liberal anti-family agenda while seeing itself as seeking a more inclusive Scotland. Both caricatures have enough of a grain of truth to be credible, and the temptation (for either churches or parliament) is to retreat into a defensive bunker, or to renew the power struggle represented by the statue of John Knox on the doorstep of parliament.

It has been said that, even before this debate, devolution made the Catholic Church in Scotland feel somewhat threatened (over issues such as denominational schools) by a dominant culture perceived perhaps as culturally Presbyterian, or Protestant, or secular. And if the Church of Scotland's view was more confident, that confidence may have been disturbed, at least for the more conservative proportion of its membership, by the Clause 2a repeal. All established institutions are likely to feel threatened by change, by the appearance of new institutions and by realignment of power; the extent to which new patterns are emerging from scratch around the parliament will undoubtedly undermine those whose security is built on the capital of the past. Authority and credibility may have to be earned, in new ways.

It is not so much that the Kirk's General Assembly has been displaced from its claimed role as the nearest thing we used to have to a parliament, but that the passion and fervour which the people of Scotland had for its debates at the time of the Disruption seem to belong to another world. Perhaps such changes open up the possibility for Assembly and Church to be what they should be. It has been observed that, in Ireland for example, the growth of 'secularism', by challenging a dominant religious culture, may paradoxically have helped other faith communities to play a fuller part in the life of the nation, and even enabled the formerly dominant church to clarify its own mission. Certainly, the parliament has been keen at least to pay lip service to the contribution of other faith communities to Scotland, through Time for Reflection and in other ways.

This involvement of Scotland's various faith communities in leading what was famously described as 'proportional praying' in the parliament has not been universally welcomed. For some, it represents another example of political correctness – a concept which in itself might repay deeper theological analysis. Some of what falls under that rubric profoundly challenges historical blind spots in Christian ethics (for example, over racism); some constitutes a new ethical orthodoxy, at least among those in political power, which is sometimes at odds with traditional Christian understanding; and some may represent a descent into a new petty moralism more focused on language than on action. The rise of the right in other parts of Europe, building on resentment and prejudice, suggests that putting some issues beyond public debate may have consequences that are quite the opposite of what is intended.

Whether the language of 'secularisation' has any meaning or not, and whether the changes to which it normally refers are welcomed as liberating or resisted as threatening, the place of the churches in Scotland today is clearly not what it was. In that respect, the coming of the parliament may be seen as a watershed. Most of the books which analysed the movement which brought the parliament into being refer to the contribution of the churches to that process, most conspicuously in the Constitutional Convention. Few of the works which have analysed Scotland one year into the new parliamentary era or the new millennium refer to the churches at all; those that do note the views on sexuality of a church leader (the late Cardinal Winning) and a prominent Christian businessman (Brian Soutar), and little else. The implication might be that churches which had a role in articulating a wide political agenda have either been confined to or have retreated into a narrower focus. Such writing, of course, comes mainly from an academic or political perspective – but that does not diminish its significance (especially when the Kirk itself proclaims that it has lost the right to be heard in public debate). There may also be a generational issue here. A parliament whose average age is well under 50 has many members from a generation in which participation in the churches – particularly the larger churches – is dramatically reduced.

Of course, we can respond that the Church of Scotland still has more active elders than the Labour Party has individual members in Scotland. But the perception of decline translates into actions that limit both status and influence. If we are playing a power game, then the churches are losing. And one reaction to that in the churches may be a retreat into a more inward-looking approach focused on the churches' 'core business' and leaving politics to the politicians.

However, the opportunity which the Scottish Churches Parliamentary Office was designed to help the churches take is to play a part in an active civic Scotland – through taking the undeniably greater opportunities the parliament is giving, through the (slowly) emerging Civic Forum, and through the development of other forms of creative engagement. It is hoped that this can be done without the co-option suggested by one of the many polls conducted on parliament's first year, which found that those most sympathetic to the parliament were those most closely involved in working with it.

Such a need for reassessment is not unique to the churches. It may be significant to review developments with four of the key institutions of civic Scotland prior to devolution – alongside the churches (together, through ACTS) in many bodies were the local authorities (together, through CoSLA), the unions (together, through STUC) and the voluntary sector (together, through SCVO). Two years later, CoSLA seemed to be on the verge of unravelling, and the STUC had a lower profile and seemed increasingly confined to its 'home territory' of industrial relations and economic issues, although SCVO (perhaps representing a younger generation of civic action) had become an increasingly key player. The number of MSPs with experience of the voluntary sector, along with the 'third way' thinking that seeks alternatives to the public-vs-private debates of the past, gives this 'third force' considerable prominence in this parliament and beyond it in the emerging Scotland; and it is here that the churches may increasingly locate themselves.

If this recognition of the voluntary sector is to be more than lip service, we need to make our contribution credible and effective; like supporters of small football teams, we need to allow for the possibility that, in a small country, the players may not only hear what we are shouting, but might even do what we say. Abuse from the touchline (whether it sounds like a sermon or a scolding *Guardian* editorial) is therefore not enough.

The starting point for both credibility and contribution must lie in the range and depth of experience of the churches in every kind of community in Scotland, backed up by a solid tradition of thinking that experience through into public policy. And a new, pluralist Scotland will be well served if we contribute from our faith and the vision that is bound up with it – not because a proof text will demonstrate that God is on our side, but because we are giving our best and expect others to do that too. In order to do that, however, we need to learn how to sing the Lord's song in a strange new land, to discover what God is doing in all of this.

Theologically, we need to recognise that such a contribution may be more effectively made from the margins. The Church of Scotland at least has been comfortably part of the Scottish establishment, not only institutionally but also because many of the key players in the other arms of the establishment have been elders or active members. If that is becoming less the case (although there are still around a dozen MSPs who are Kirk elders – ten times the number which would be proportional in a random sample of the population), a church that feels pushed to the margins of power might have distinctive things to say. Though institutionally weaker in areas of deprivation (urban and rural), churches remain actively engaged in these communities, doing some of their most exciting work in genuine partnership. This is not as fully recognised by the Scottish Executive (either in documents like the regeneration strategy or in funding terms) as is the case in England – probably reflecting a religious scene complicated by sectarianism and seen as a minefield by many politicians, despite increasing ecumenical working through the Scottish Churches Community Trust.

If we can be sensitive to what we hear in the contexts where the brave new Scotland is hurting, churches can use the opportunities we still have to be one of the channels through which these voices can be heard: not so much opening our mouths for the voiceless but helping ensure that those who have been made dumb by the politics of power can find a voice. It was the churches who first brought an asylum-seeker to give evidence to a parliamentary committee, reflecting our work on the ground; perhaps that and the efforts of the churches to engage with the victims of the 2001 foot-and-mouth epidemic may represent one model of how to do this.

If the parliament's beginnings reflected any one personal influence, it must surely have been that of its first First Minister, Donald Dewar. The character of the Scottish parliament reflects much of the integrity and drive of that 'conspicuously cultural Presbyterian' who fathered it, and the events and many words in the aftermath of his death clearly reaffirmed (in a parliament that had been criticised for lacking an infectious vision for the new Scotland) social justice at the heart of its agenda. His successor also took the occasion of parliament's third anniversary to renew the Scottish Executive's commitment to social justice.

It is not simply that the Scottish Labour Party seems more comfortable with the language of social justice, but that the political centre of gravity in the parliament reflects a key part of the dynamic of the movement out of which it was born. During the Thatcher years, Scotland came to seem more and more out of kilter with the 'me' culture that was being grown, to an extent that made the Conservatives' majority in the Scotland of the 1950s a distant memory. There is some statistical backing for the 'guid conceit of ourselves' that suggested that we were committed to a more caring society than appeared to be the broad view of 'middle England'. Scots apparently continue to be more prone to looking to the public sector for solutions, and open to policies of redistribution, than is the case in England. Recent research suggests that this continues to be so, but that the political system through which we express these views is now significantly different.[1]

Symbolically, the arrangement of our parliament has Labour in the middle ground, with the largest opposition party generally to their left (their coalition partners shifted, mid-term, from left to right, though probably not with any great symbolism). If governments are pulled towards their opposition in search of the middle ground, Labour in Scotland is pulled in the opposite direction from the pressure on the Westminster government. Although there were signs that the SNP may have been more reluctant in the run-up to the election to enter into the spending commitments of every popular left-wing cause, political debate in the early years of the parliament was substantially about whether the Executive was going far enough or fast enough towards targets of social justice, rather than about reining them in or changing direction.

The context for a social theology in Scotland today, then, is one in which a legacy of 'cultural Presbyterianism', in the form of a commitment to social justice, is at the heart of parliament's and perhaps the nation's agenda; in which there is an openness to hearing voices from the margins and from groups that have traditionally been far from power; and in which the range of voluntary-sector bodies that help make up 'civic Scotland' are making an increasingly significant contribution. Even in this, the second least multicultural nation in Europe (only Iceland is less ethnically diverse), a dominant culture in the new Scotland has not yet emerged from the diversity; perhaps we are still growing up, but what emerges will not be the Scotland of John Knox or even one in which the Christendom capital of cultural Presbyterianism is as embedded. While the heady optimism of the build-up to the parliament has given way to the more limited (humble?) ambition of Jack McConnell's 'do less but do it better', there are successes and frustrations. Perhaps, as we in the churches look at a new institution which seems to spend too much money on buildings, which says brave new things about how it will operate but reverts to well-worn patterns, which talks a good game about justice and the poor but often lacks the courage to put resources where its words are, whose most public 'servants' bring commitment that somehow gets frittered away in wrong directions, and who can even decide their own pay increases, we might glimpse something familiar. The theological challenge is to recognise where God's purpose is working itself out, in and beyond the parliament, and to bear witness with the same passionate, prophetic and pastoral commitment to the commonweal of Scotland as the man whose statue is on parliament's doorstep.

Holyrood was, symbolically, the last place of sanctuary in Scotland – a place, on the margins, to turn to for those who had nowhere else to go. Parliament's much debated future home is usually pronounced to rhyme with Hollywood (which, along with 'hollered', is what Bill Gates' spell-checker offers to substitute for it!). If we are serious about it being closer to the place of the Cross, we need to remember that the place of the Cross was where the power politicians of the Holy City did their dirty business, where we discover just how destructive the self-righteous power of church and state can be when they get together, and where we hear Christ saying: 'Father, forgive them, they don't know what they are doing.'

Note

1. Lindsay Paterson and others, *New Scotland, New Politics?*, Edinburgh: Edinburgh University Press, 2001, ch. 8 passim.

Part II

Doing Social Theology: Working with Traditions

It is by no means self-apparent that Christian theology has a relevant social contribution in this day and age. The many shades of beliefs and commitments in a society such as Scotland make for a situation where it would seem that consumerism – what we are prepared to buy into – may be all that unites us. While we may with reason suspect that this precisely is what we are meant to think, for the sake of profit margins, at the same time the advocates of 'post-modernism' argue that we are beyond the days of grand, overarching theories; the days of ordering and controlling are long since over. In times past, of course, it was regularly in theological terms that unity and uniformity was given its justification. Is there then any room nowadays for claims to insight and truth and wisdom from a theological starting point? The two chapters by Professors Sagovsky and Forrester pursue the question of whether and how theological work, whether based around natural law or in evangelical (biblical) terms, may still have something to offer.

   The tradition of natural law is long and distinguished, although its historic course in Protestant Scotland began to crumble in the eighteenth century. Intriguingly, however, and though shorn of its traditional terms of

language, something akin to natural law has survived
not least in the formulation of the notion of human
rights. It has to be recognised that this is only a starting
point, since the applications of such thinking are a matter
for casework – or, classically, *epiekeia* or equity – but
the implication nevertheless is that the tradition still has
life in it, and therefore also a point of contact with
theological reflection. Chapter 3 on 'Natural Law and
Social Theology' traces the history and delves briefly into
the possible future of such an exchange. The suggestion
clearly is that the quest for universals is not entirely
hopeless and may provide an important basis not only
for social philosophising but also for social theology.

The twentieth-century theologian Karl Barth was
notoriously suspicious of natural theology; and, as his
work is drawn on in Chapter 4, with the title 'The
Political Service of Theology in Scotland', there is pre-
dictably less optimism here in the natural-law approach.
It is argued that, whether by challenge or in correction
or simply by complementary insights, a christological
input is indispensable if theology which is Christian is to
be of service in the contemporary world. At the same
time, the difficulty to be acknowledged with this more
evangelical approach, as with natural law indeed, is that
there has been a history of distortions and partialities,
and a veritable contest of interpretation continues to this
day. The hope must be for a sourcing of both vision and
prophetic insight – that is, a looking to a better future
and an understanding in the particular of what must
change – but due humility would counsel the theologian
to quarry something in the nature of fragments or morsels
here, rather than supposing an ability to assume knowledge of any finally comprehensive conclusions.

Although there are obviously issues unresolved in the
crossover between the two chapters, there is some inter-

esting and important common ground. The interpretation of tradition and its continuing validity is a shared concern within the project, and a challenge to those who would say the past should be laid aside. Furthermore, while these chapters are wary of the dangers of so-called metanarratives – grand discourses, whether of communism or the Aryan race, or also of democracy and freedom and progress which historically have had oppressive outcomes when the lust for power has taken over – the authors persist in looking for truths applicable to our common humanity. Sagovsky's chapter stops with the discussion of how we might talk about how it matters humanly to be alive; Forrester treads deeper into ecclesiology and politics, that is to say, what positively the church might hope to embody and contribute for the sake of social and individual well-being.

The intention then, is – in spite of understandable controversy – to detect whether through natural-law reasoning or through biblical interpretation, or no doubt some combination of these, there might be a distinctively theological perception of human community and flourishing. The debate will no doubt continue!

I have focused upon central features of the Scottish philosophical tradition, in particular its emphasis on realism, or 'common sense' . . . I believe that [this] philosophy occupies, and for many centuries has occupied, a central place in Scottish culture. This point is crucial, for nothing sustains a people's sense of cultural identity as much as does its knowledge of its cultural roots . . . The philosophy of this country is rooted in world philosophy. It is fed by it and feeds into it, and is *one of the great success stories of world culture*. It matters to us, and contributing as it still does to the wider philosophical scene, it matters also far beyond Scotland.

Alexander Broadie,
from *Why Scottish Philosophy Matters*

3

Natural Law and Social Theology

Nicholas Sagovsky

Introduction: Scotland and the 'Natural Law' Tradition

A 'social theology', I take it, seeks to give a critical account of the presence and will of God in human social and political activity. Is God at work immanently in all such human interaction? Should God be seen more as the transcendent judge of human activity? What theological rationale can be given for the involvement of Christians in public issues? What are Christians involved in social and political issues seeking to achieve? The central question for a social theology is, surely, the question of God's justice.

An Englishman who looks at contemporary Scottish social theology might well expect to see as the dominant motif 'Christ against culture'.[1] The received view is one of principled Reformed commitment to the realisation of God's just reign hammered out in historic opposition to political and ecclesiastical compromise. The Westminster Confession takes a radical, Augustinian view of the Fall as the catastrophic eclipse of the human capacity for justice both individually (hence the need for 'justification by faith') and socially (only on the basis of revealed, Scriptural truth can human beings construct a truly just society). Fallen human beings need to be redeemed from sin, and to be sustained in truth by the gift of the Holy Spirit which comes through faith in Christ alone. Barth's theology was welcomed in Scotland (where it has remained continuously in print) because it reaffirmed the Reformed emphases on the priority of the Word, the rejection of theological compromise, and the need for 'the Church to be the Church'. For Barth, pitching himself against those who used the name of Christ to affirm the liberal culture of Germany in 1914, and then against the nationalist culture of Nazi Germany, the development of a social theology by a national church, such as the Church of Scotland, would indeed be a perilous enterprise.

Nevertheless, it is one that Scottish Calvinist theologians have readily undertaken, building on a theologically based understanding of 'natural law'. The Westminster Confession famously asserts that 'the light of nature, and the works of creation and providence do so far manifest the goodness, wisdom, and power of God as to leave men unexcusable . . .' (I.1), and that 'God created man, male and female, . . . having the law of God written in their hearts'; and the *Larger Catechism* (1648) asserts that 'The moral law is the declaration of the will of God to mankind, directing and binding everyone to personal, perfect and perpetual conformity and obedience to it'.[2] Alasdair MacIntyre has shown that, for Scottish Calvinist thinkers in the seventeenth and early eighteenth centuries, an emphasis on 'the light of nature' and 'the moral law' was readily combined with a thriving Aristotelianism to produce an integrated, theologically based account of natural human knowledge, both moral and scientific. He speaks of 'that Scottish tradition in which the fundamental concerns of philosophy, Scots law, and presbyterian theology were inseparable'; where philosophy *'in conjunction with theology'* was seen as 'the discipline whose enquiries provide the rational justification for the metaphysical and moral principles constitutive of the political and social order'.[3] Between the Reformation and the Enlightenment, there was a lively interaction between Scotland and the Netherlands, where thinkers in the tradition of Grotius (1583–1645) and Pufendorf (1632–94) were working in a similar way. Only in the latter part of the eighteenth century did this Scottish tradition of knowledge according to a theologically grounded understanding of 'natural law', largely because its normative Aristotelian presuppositions were no longer serviceable, mutate into increasingly secularised forms of Enlightenment rationalism from which Calvinist thinkers separated themselves totally.

This turning away from lively discussion of 'the natural' and of 'the moral law' in the Church of Scotland of the late eighteenth century left the thinkers of the Scottish Enlightenment to develop their ideas in the political and social fields freed of engagement with the best that theological thinking had to offer. Elements of the once-integrated 'natural law' tradition continued in the commonsense moral philosophy of Thomas Reid and Dugald Stewart[4] and the social theology of Thomas Chalmers,[5] but it was no longer buttressed by lively Aristotelianism. Theologians largely left the field of 'natural theology' to incipiently rationalist thinkers like Adam Smith and David Hume. The contemporary social vision of the Church of Scotland (or simply of Scotland) owes more, I guess, to the socialist thought of the nineteenth century, forged in the midst of huge economic inequality and social injustice, than to the Aristotelianism of the eighteenth. Both socialism and Aristotelianism, however, share a concern for the flourishing of the individual within the community, though they would give differing accounts of how that is to be achieved historically. Where socialism is committed to forms of secular eschatology, the teleological strand in Aristotelianism ensures a continuing commitment to some form of thinking in terms of 'natural law'. Though Catholicism has been the one Christian tradition consistently characterised by Aristotelian theological method, there is in principle no reason why contemporary Reformed theology should not benefit from encounter with the socially and politically radical neo-Aristotelian thinking of writers like Finnis,[6] Nussbaum[7] and MacIntyre. With the newly re-established Scottish parliament now beginning to flex its muscles in socially radical ways, this is a good time to be asking about the foundation and method of a social theology that can bring together the Church of Scotland and the other Scottish churches in critical engagement with the political process. It seems to me that the socialist emphases on the hope of social transformation, the importance of the common good, the redistribution of wealth in favour of the poor, and the subsidiary role of the state can only be enriched by being brought together with aspects of the Aristotelian tradition: the characteristically 'thick' descriptions of human needs and human flourishing, together with the emphasis on practical rationality and the common good. Furthermore, none of this comes into conflict with the testimony of Scripture.

My contribution, as an English Anglican, to a Scottish symposium, which seeks to reassess the possibility of a social theology for contemporary Scotland, will be to suggest that there needs to be much less suspicion of 'natural theology' as a complement to the theology that is explicitly grounded on the tradition of the Scriptures, and that the lively tradition of natural theology which existed within the Calvinism of the Church of Scotland needs to be revived. In sketching how it thrived and was then to a degree lost, I shall be heavily reliant on the story told by Alasdair MacIntyre in *Whose Justice? Which Rationality?*, but, in pointing to an area where it might flourish again, I shall take a contemporary example: the implementation of the Human Rights Act, which was embedded in the legislation that brought into being the Scottish parliament.

What is Meant by 'Natural Law'? Christian Tradition to the Reformation

The fundamental claim of 'natural law' thinking is that there is a 'rightness' about certain modes of human action, both individual and social, which therefore make for human flourishing. This 'rightness' can be read merely negatively (there are certain given constraints upon human action) or positively (there are certain actions in which human beings ought to engage). It can be read cognitively (human beings know that this is the case) or non-cognitively (human beings find out *through their action* that this is the case) or as an admixture of these positions. What is characteristic of this tradition is its universalism: it asserts something that is true for all human beings. It has been developed in Western tradition largely through forms of Aristotelianism, where it has been associated with teleological understandings of human nature (much attacked in the nineteenth century, and now said by some to be quite untenable), the priority of the rational over the emotional (which was Nietzsche's point of attack), and the unity of recognisable human 'good' rather than a diversity of chosen human 'goods' (which is a keynote of liberalism and a plural society, defended by thinkers like Isaiah Berlin).

The origins of the Christian 'natural law' tradition must be traced back both to classical sources and to the Scriptures.[8] Plato was profoundly interested in the 'right ordering' of his ideal city. He sought by intuition to discern what was the best *politeia*, or constitutional life, of a republic which was to be a model society. He extrapolated from the life of Athens as he knew it to an ideal order in human society (an order of 'justice') which formed the basis for his *Laws*. His pupil Aristotle adopted the inductive method of looking at human societies and comparing their constitutions, choosing which among them best conformed to the 'nature' of human beings. His *Ethics* discusses the virtues that will be cultivated when human beings live rationally according to their nature; his *Politics* ('man is, by nature, a political animal') gives his account of how human societies should be structured and should function in accord with 'the nature' of human society.

In Stoic thought, such reflection on the 'nature' of cities, people and the world was universalised. Cicero (106–43 BCE) wrote that 'True law is right reason in agreement with Nature; it is of universal application, unchanging and everlasting; it summons to duty by its commands, and averts from wrongdoing by its prohibitions'.[9] From him comes the phrase 'natural law' (*lex naturalis*). This theme is taken up by Marcus Aurelius: 'Remembering always what World-Nature is, and what my own nature is, and how the one stands in respect to the other – so small a fraction of so vast a Whole – bear in mind that no man can hinder you from conforming each word and deed to that Nature of which you are a part.'[10]

The Scriptural root of the term 'natural law' lies in Romans 2:14: 'When the Gentiles who have not the law do *by nature* what the law requires, they are a law to themselves, even though they do not have the law. They show that what the law requires is written on their hearts.' The thrust of Paul's argument is directed towards the Jews who have the law (Torah) and do not keep it. His point is that 'it is not the hearers of the law who are righteous before God, but the doers of the law who shall be justified'. By mentioning, in passing, Gentiles who 'do by nature what the law requires', he raises the question as to what norms or principles guide Gentiles who act in this way and where those practical norms come from. All he says is that 'They show that what the law requires is written on their hearts, while their conscience also bears witness and their conflicting thoughts accuse or perhaps excuse them' (Romans 2:15). The inference was readily drawn that, when Paul talked about the Gentiles doing 'by nature what the law requires', his words were in accord with Cicero's language about *lex naturalis* (natural law).

There were other Scriptural themes which supported this discernment of a 'natural law' known to all. By no means all references to the law in the Old Testament need be taken to refer to the written Torah. If there were a 'natural law', a meditation like that in Psalm 19 could easily be read as one which spoke of the law in this wider, universal sense:

> The law of the Lord is perfect,
>   reviving the soul.
> the testimony of the Lord is sure
>   making wise the simple;
> the precepts of the Lord are right
>   rejoicing the heart.
>
>   (Psalm 19:7–8)

According to Amos, the nations are judged (Amos 1:3–2:3) because they do not observe what they know of the 'law of the Lord' which is immanent throughout all creation (cf. Psalm 148:1–6). The judgment of the sheep and the goats in Matthew 25 in which God reveals precisely who has cared for the needy and who has not (Matthew 25:31–46) takes place when 'all the nations' are assembled, and so presumably applies to 'all the nations' (cf. Romans 2:16).

St John Chrysostom (c. 347–407) summed up the thinking of the early church when he wrote: 'In creating man at the beginning, God placed within him a natural law.'[11] Augustine, who drew heavily on the thought of Cicero, distinguished between the 'eternal law', according to which God providentially governed his creation in accordance with the eternal and immutable ideas in his mind,[12] and the 'temporal law' by which particular communities are governed. The precepts of the 'eternal law' are impressed on human minds by the Creator, so they are experienced as 'natural law'. In *On Grace and Free Will*, he explains that 'natural law' teaches (as Plato taught) that the passions and the 'spirited' parts of the soul ought to be subject to reason and reason to God.[13]

God was seen as both law-giver and creator, ruler and judge. An integrated understanding of God as law-giver, of 'natural law' and of 'revealed law', was enormously important to the developing Christian tradition. It was well grounded in Scripture and it engaged with contemporary social practice. There was in the West, with its well-developed tradition of Roman law, a powerful interest in God as the one who established creation according to his own law; who rules according to his own law; and who will judge according to his own law. With the Christianisation of Europe, Roman law was increasingly adopted along with a Christian theological framework. It was presupposed that the positive law of Christian nations should reflect the justice of God's eternal law and that Roman law provided a sound basis for this.

Roman lawyers spoke in terms of *ius naturale* (natural law) and *ius civile* (civil law), which could be roughly approximated to God's law and human law. Ulpian (d. 228), who is known only because he is quoted by Justinian (c. 482–565), distinguished *ius naturale*, which for him is what nature teaches all animals, from the *ius gentium* (the law of the nations). The *ius gentium* was the law common to all peoples, the law of a 'common humanity' which all people could be expected to observe. Ulpian made a threefold distinction: 'natural law', 'the law of nations' and 'positive law'. This distinction of *ius naturale*, *ius gentium* and *ius civile*, which is also found in Justinian, was taken into the mainstream of medieval thought, where it was supplemented by reference to the 'eternal law' of God and to the law of Israel.

It was Thomas Aquinas (c. 1225–74) who made the classic synthesis which is still influential today. He distinguished the *eternal law* by which God governed the universe; the *positive divine law* revealed first in the Old and then in the New Testament; the *natural law* according to which norms for human moral conduct could be discerned by all those who wished to do so; and *positive human law*, which comprised the 'civil law' according to which individual states are governed and 'the law of nations' according to which the interrelations of states and peoples are governed. Positive (human) law must accord with the requirements of natural law. Natural law was for him so instilled into people's minds 'as to be known by nature' ('*Deus eam mentibus hominum inseruit naturaliter cognoscendam*').[14] He speaks of it as the rational creature's 'participation in the eternal law' ('*talis participatio legis aeternae in rationali creatura lex naturalis dicitur*').[15] Thomas believes that all human beings have by nature some genuine access to the mind of God. To some degree they know, and can rationally reflect upon, what God wills for them, both individually and socially. Quite separate are the questions as to whether or to what extent they are able to act on such knowledge; as to whether such knowledge or such action is salvific; as to how such knowledge relates to the knowledge of God's law that comes through Scripture. The assertion is solely that human beings do indeed, by virtue of their created humanity, know something of God's will for them both individually and corporately. It can, however, be expanded to the claim that Christian theologians or the church are indeed able, on the basis of their secure knowledge of God's law, to discern in those things that matter to God whether or not human actions are in accordance with 'what the law requires' (i.e. the will of God), and in controverted instances to reason intelligently (theologically) about this.

The clerical interest in law, fostered in Western theology by the rich inheritance of Roman juridical thinking, was in part responsible for the reaction of the Reformers against all forms of legalism. The oppositions in Lutheranism between Gospel and law, between grace and nature, and between Scripture and philosophy (especially Aristotelian philosophy), challenged the place of 'natural law' as a vehicle for the salvific knowledge of God. Nevertheless, despite his strong sense of the dialectic of grace, Luther still retained a firm belief in the importance of natural law for social order and general knowledge of God's will. For Calvin, whose thought is less confrontational and more systematic than

Luther's, the question of the 'natural' knowledge of God is handled less dialectically.[16] He held that the knowledge of God has been naturally implanted in minds (*Inst.* 1.3) but that 'the natural gifts were corrupted in man through sin' (*Inst.* 2.2.12). The gifts of reason, of discriminating right from wrong, and the love of truth were not, however, totally destroyed. Calvin quotes Aristotle with approval: 'Man is by nature a social animal' (*Inst.* 2.2.13), and goes on to say:

> No man can be found who does not understand that every sort of human organization must be regulated by laws, and who does not comprehend the principles of those laws. Hence arise the unvarying consent of all nations and of individual mortals with regard to laws. *For their seeds have, without teacher or lawgiver, been implanted in all men.*[17]

He goes on to speak of 'a universal apprehension of reason and understanding by nature implanted in men' (*Inst.* 2.2.14), and to quote Romans 2:14–15, before defining natural (i.e. moral) law: 'Natural law is that apprehension of the conscience which distinguishes sufficiently between just and unjust, and which deprives men of the excuse of ignorance, while it proves them guilty by their own testimony' (*Inst.* 2.2.22).

We need to review at this point the claim that was being made by thinkers like Aquinas and Calvin. It is strictly limited: that the 'law' of God or the 'will' of God is in general terms known to human beings by virtue of their creation. All human beings, without further revelation, have access to some understanding of God's will for them and for society, that is, we would say, to the 'moral law'. From this foundational conviction, human beings may proceed to develop moral teaching and systems of laws that are in broad accord with the will of God. When they have the Scripture, and their moral teaching and law-making is explicitly informed by Scriptural teaching, they can be assured that their moral teaching and law-making is in conformity with the law of God; and in controverted situations, by the application of reason in accord with the guidance of the Holy Spirit, they can develop new teaching and new laws in accord with the will and the law of God.

The Understanding of 'Natural Law' at the Time of the Scottish Enlightenment

Alasdair MacIntyre has written about 'a systematic, even if unstable, blend of Calvinism and Aristotelianism' in seventeenth-century Scotland, exemplifying this from *The Institutions of the Law of Scotland* by Sir James Dalrymple of Stair, first published in 1681.[18] Stair's comprehensive account of the basis of Scottish law is grounded in the theology of the Westminster Confession:

> Man being sent into the World to behold the Works of God, and to Glorifie him, for doing whereof, he hath some Rules written in his heart by the Law of Nature, and in the Word of God, and for the rest is allowed to do as he conceiveth most conducible thereto, *that whether he eat, or drink, or whatsoever else he do, he do all to the glory of God.*[19]

In equating Divine Law ('that mainly which is Written in Man's heart') with the Law of Nature, Stair quotes Romans 2:14:

> [This] is called the Law of Nature, because it is known Naturally, either immediately, like unto these Instincts which are in the other Creatures, whereby they know what is necessary for their preservation: so the first Principles of this Natural Law are known to men, without Reasoning or Experience, without Art, Industry or Education, and so

are known to men every where through the World . . . Such are the common practical Principles that God is to be obeyed, Parents honoured, our selves defended, violence repulsed, Children to be loved, educate [sic] and provided for.[20]

He goes on to assert that, besides giving to human beings these practical principles to live by, God has also gifted them with Reason: 'that thence they might by consequence deduce his Law in more particular Cases'. Stair develops an integrated account of justice, divine (Scriptural) law, natural law, reason, conscience and equity. His account of natural law is grounded not only in the Scriptures, but also in Roman law and in Aristotelian moral anthropology. To a modern reader, the echoes of Aquinas are as striking as those of Calvin:

The Law of Nature, as it is impressed on our hearts; so in the Goodness of God, it is expressed in his Word, wherein he hath not only holden forth those sacred mysteries which could only be known by Revelation, as having no Principle in Nature from whence they are deducible; but also, because through Sin and Evil Custom, the Natural Law in man's Heart was much defaced, disordered, and erroneously deduced: he hath therefore Re-printed the Law of Nature in a viv[id]er Character in the Scripture . . . The Analogie of the Law of Nature, even in the Hearts of Heathens, and as it is set down in the Law of God, evidenceth sufficiently, that both of them proceed from the same Omniscient Author.[21]

On the basis of this 'analogy', Stair went on to develop his account of Scottish law; on the same basis there developed a lively tradition of moral philosophy.

MacIntyre argues that the task of a professor of moral philosophy in eighteenth-century Scotland came to be 'that of providing a defence of just those fundamental moral principles, conceived of as antecedent to both all positive law and all peculiar forms of social organization, which defined peculiarly Scottish institutions and attitudes'.[22] It was to just such a defence of 'natural law', meaning the self-evident first principles of morality, law, science and social organisation in general, that Francis Hutcheson, who became professor of moral philosophy in Glasgow in 1730, devoted his life. Hutcheson opens his *System of Moral Philosophy* by asserting:

> The intention of moral philosophy is to direct men to that course of action which tends most effectually to promote their greatest happiness and perfection; as far as it can be done by observations and conclusions discoverable from the constitution of nature, without any aid of supernatural revelation: these maxims or rules of conduct are therefore reputed as laws of nature, and the system for collection of them is called the Law of Nature.[23]

God appears shortly afterwards simply as 'the Author of Nature'. Hutcheson also writes of God as the governor of the universe and of 'the sole use of words, or writing, in laws' as 'to discover the will of the governor'. He deals first with 'positive laws' which 'must by such means be discovered'; but he goes on to argue:

> There is another and primary way by which God discovers his will concerning our conduct ... even by the constitution of nature, and the powers of reason, and moral perception, which he has given to mankind, and thus reveals a law with its sanctions, as effectively as by words, or writing; and in a manner more noble and divine.[24]

Hutcheson's best-known pupil was Adam Smith, whose work continues to show the hallmark of the Scottish school of moral philosophy: its integration with a Calvinist, theological basis through a conception of 'natural law'. In *The Theory of Moral Sentiments* (1759),

Smith sought to demonstrate (as had Calvin) that the existence and observance of general rules are necessary to sustain the social state. He writes eloquently of the need for justice in human society:

> Justice . . . is the main pillar that upholds the whole edifice. If it is removed, the great, the immense fabric of human society, that fabric which to raise and support seems in this world, if I may say so, to have been the peculiar and darling care of Nature, must in a moment crumble into atoms.[25]

However, Smith does not specify precise precepts of a universal moral law. In his refusal to follow the Aristotelian tradition which specified particular human virtues, he and his friend David Hume were much influenced by Montesquieu[26] and the beginnings of a sense of the tension between the 'goods' adopted in different societies. What Smith did hold on to was the conviction that certain desires are implanted in human beings by the 'Author of Nature' and that through the exercise of these desires a rational (divine) plan, whose purposes are not always known to humans, is unfolded in the world. Here he was echoing Newton's mechanistic, deistic cosmology, by which he was much impressed, and which he sought to develop in the field of human social interaction. Skinner suggests it is characteristic of Smith to argue that some aspects of human nature require certain sorts of control, while others ensure that such controls do in fact develop:

> Smith . . . suggests that social order becomes possible by virtue of the restraints which individuals impose upon *themselves*, thus unfolding at least part of a Divine Plan, a Plan which is given substantial expression by virtue of the activities of individuals who are quite unconscious of the end which these activities help to promote.[27]

This is a shadowy relic of 'natural law', which Smith went on to retain behind the magisterial economic thought of *The Wealth of Nations* (1776). Smith's interest in ethics, economics and political philosophy was all of a piece, and it all retained an integrating, but much-loosened, framework of 'natural law'. A major shift had, however, taken place, under cover of this residual 'natural law' framework. Smith moved away from Hutcheson's privileging of forms of altruism (which was common to all forms of 'natural law' thinking to this point) towards the privileging of personal passions. His reference to an 'Invisible hand' in *The Theory of the Moral Sentiments* (IV.i.10) and *The Wealth of Nations* (IV.2.9) is a brief reminder of his attenuated hold on natural law and his optimistic claim that, in the fulfilment of the desires that motivate human wills, we shall somehow, mysteriously, do the will of God.

Smith is a crucial mediating figure in the attenuation of 'natural law' thinking and in the shift of focus to economic and political 'scientism'. Still more radical was the epistemological critique of his contemporary, David Hume, whose published work, according to MacIntyre, 'presented a series of the profoundest challenges to and ruptures with the fundamental convictions which had been embodied in the dominant Scottish tradition'.[28] MacIntyre develops a detailed account of the ways in which Hume's critique of moral reasoning was 'deeply at odds with the Calvinist Aristotelians of the Scottish seventeenth century'. Under the pressure of his sceptical questioning about causality, teleology and rationality, the tradition of the unified exercise of practical reason in constructive public debate was seriously undermined. It took time for the revolution to work through, but the unified tradition of Protestant theological Aristotelianism collapsed. It gave place to the deontological Kantianism and the pragmatic rationalism of the Enlightenment, and to the 'commonsense' philosophy of Thomas Reid and others who fought a rearguard action in defence of innate moral knowledge, and to the positing on theological grounds of the 'moral law' by evangelical Christians like Thomas Chalmers. When Protestant Christians lost their confidence in the shared apprehension and deployment of 'natural law' in the public domain, however energetic they might be in the social and political exercise of charitable works, they were at a severe disadvantage in developing political and social theologies which engaged broadly with the needs of Scottish society. So far as I can discern, throughout the nineteenth and twentieth centuries, there was in Scottish theology no revival of the Calvinist tradition of moral philosophy based upon 'natural law'.

The Human Rights Act and 'Natural Law'

It is nevertheless rightly claimed in the Report of the Church and Nation Committee of the Church of Scotland (2000) that 'The classical Reformed attitude towards the civil authorities might be described as one of "critical support". This support is theologically grounded in frequent reference to Romans 13, 1 Peter 2 and Old Testament models of kingship.'[29] We might see this, rather crudely, as 'top-down support' in the Augustinian tradition for civil authorities who are expected to act in broad accord with the revealed will of God, principally by restraining wrongdoing. What a positive 'social theology' would look for is 'bottom-up' support for the discernment in society of developments that are in accord with the will of God, known through 'natural law'. Looked at this way, one can see why a contemporary social theology is much less likely to come from the supposedly benign, but actually competitive, individualism of the later Smith (moderated though it was by a concern for social provision[30]) than the transformative socialism of the nineteenth century. The Report does, indeed, note the general duty of the church to promote the welfare of the State, which is clearly expressed in the Articles Declaratory of 1921, but the question remains as to how, and on what theological basis, this is to be done. It seems to me that, without a strong doctrine of 'natural law' at the centre of a Christian social theology, the distinctive role of the Church of Scotland in 'critical support' of those with power to bring about a more just and inclusive society is much weakened, and that a suitably flexible, but Scripturally grounded, doctrine of natural law could provide an undergirding for ecumenical co-operation such as that called for in the Church and Nation Committee Report and experienced, for example, in the Jubilee 2000 campaign. It is against the background of this need for a strong mode of theological argument, central to which is a commitment to 'natural law', that we can draw out the positive implications of the Human Rights Act (1998) for the development of a Scottish social theology.

The Human Rights Act (1998), which takes the European Convention on Human Rights (1953) into British law, is clearly developed from the secular, universalist tradition which stems from the Universal Declaration of Human Rights (1948). It is by no means rooted in older, Thomistic and Calvinist notions of 'right'. The UDHR was drafted in the immediate aftermath of a war in which the systematic brutality of which human beings are capable had been exposed for all to see. There was a deep feeling that the Holocaust above all had infringed a moral anthropology which should be universally self-evident: what had been done to Jews, political prisoners, homosexuals, gypsies and others in the camps was self-evidently wrong to all right-thinking people. The Preamble to the UDHR is a thoroughly 'modern' document in that it makes no appeal to God or 'nature' to underpin a recognition of inherent human 'dignity', 'inalienable rights' and membership of the 'human family':

> Whereas recognition of the inherent dignity and of the equal and inalienable rights of all members of the human family is the foundation of freedom, justice and peace in the world . . .[31]

The European Convention on Human Rights is an altogether slimmer document, which offers no basis for the human rights it enumerates other than by placing itself in the tradition of the UDHR:

> Considering the UDHR proclaimed by the General Assembly of the United Nations on 10th December 1948;
>   Considering that the Declaration aims at securing the universal and effective recognition and observance of the Rights therein declared . . .
>   Reaffirming the profound belief in those fundamental freedoms which are the foundation of justice and peace in the world . . .
>   The High Contracting Parties shall secure to everyone within their jurisdiction the rights and freedoms defined in Section 1 of this Convention.[32]

None of this preamble is taken into the Human Rights Act (1998), which begins its quotation from the ECHR baldly with 'Article 2: Everyone's right to life shall be protected by law'. The result is that this and the following rights are asserted without any metaphysical or traditional grounding or derivation. The Human Rights

Act simply asserts that for all human beings there is a 'right to life', a 'prohibition on torture', a 'prohibition on slavery and forced labour', a 'right to liberty and security', a 'right to a fair trial', a 'prohibition on punishment without law', a 'right to respect for privacy and family life', a 'right to freedom of thought, conscience and religion', a 'right to freedom of expression', a 'right to freedom of assembly and association', a 'right to marry and to found a family', a 'right to education' and so on. Qualifications of many of these rights are enumerated, and the list is by no means above criticism; the economic and social rights of the UDHR are strikingly omitted. Nevertheless, the very creation of this list of human rights, against which both law and administrative practice are to be judged, creates a kind of transcendental anthropology: the observance of the concomitant practices is seen to be a condition of human flourishing. Francesca Klug speaks of the bestowal of 'higher law' status on most Convention rights (i.e. the majority which are incorporated into the Human Rights Act).[33] Though the Human Rights Act leaves completely open the question as to whether these rights are 'discovered', 'recognised' or 'constructed', the fact that they are a kind of *de facto* 'higher law', operating as a norm against which positive law can be judged, suggests that we have here a thoroughly modern – potentially post-modern – development of the natural-law tradition.

Is this development one which Christians can support? In broad terms, certainly, though the affirmation of 'human rights' cannot be made uncritically. The churches were very concerned that the 'right to marry' should not put them under obligation to solemnise gay marriages, a point on which specific assurances were obtained. There may, indeed, be areas in which the jurisprudence of the

Human Rights Act develops in ways that Christians find unacceptable. Nevertheless, the overall tenor of the Act, and the list of human rights set out, is surely a celebration of 'a human being fully alive', which can be welcomed in the spirit of Irenaeus: 'The glory of God is a human being fully alive.' Here we have a list of rights, the observance of which characterises human flourishing in society. Speaking theologically, one could argue that through the traumas of modernity, especially in the twentieth century, we have come in Europe increasingly to realise that (prescinding from the question as to whether such values are implicit in some kind of social contract or more deeply embedded in human (social) nature), what it is to be a human being has to be spelt out, and infringements of the dignity of human beings have to be justiciable. The fact that a sketchy and incomplete hand-list of certain conditions for the respect of human dignity should draw close to a list that could be derived theologically within the Judeo-Christian tradition should not surprise anyone who takes the natural-law tradition seriously.

The Human Rights Act will make a major difference to legal and administrative practice. Built into the legislation which set up the Scottish parliament was the requirement that new Scottish legislation should conform to the Human Rights Act, and with this went training for civil servants in what has been called a 'human rights culture'.[34] Though the decision was taken not to set up a Human Rights Commission in England, there may well be one in Scotland. Christians will have to decide how they understand this theologically and how they respond to it practically. My suggestion is that it be seen as a wholly positive development within the tradition of natural law, and the Christian response on that basis should be fundamentally positive.

Conclusion: 'Natural Law', Theological Method and Contemporary Social Theology

I suggested at the beginning of this chapter that it is the task of a social theology to give a critical account of the presence and will of God in human political and social activity. It would be hard for Christians to argue, except in certain, specific instances, that observance of the Human Rights Act and the development of a 'human rights culture' were contrary to the will of God. There is an irony here, for the origin of modern thinking about 'human rights' lay in the opposition of thinkers like Tom Paine to the theologically based 'culture of duties' of his time, and it was in the face of strong theological opposition that a commitment to human rights has progressed. The volte-face of the Roman Catholic Church between the Syllabus of Errors (1864) and the Second Vatican Council (1962–5) is striking in this regard. Pope John XXIII's encyclical *Pacem in Terris* (1963) indicated how complete was the Catholic Church's endorsement of a whole range of human rights together with their correlative duties: 'These rights and duties', he wrote, 'derive their origin, their sustenance, and their indestructibility from the natural law.'[35] More recently, a statement from the Roman Catholic Bishops of England and Wales on the fiftieth anniversary of the Universal Declaration of Human Rights suggested that 'A properly critical understanding of human rights can offer humanity a universal moral code'.[36]

The Human Rights Act is potentially a powerful defence of the interests of the citizen against the power of the state. It has been slow to make progress in England because of the tradition of common law based on precedent, rather than the spelling-out of specific rights and duties in the Roman law tradition.[37] Furthermore, the tradition of Roman law was in its origins and ethos republican, vesting ultimate power in the Roman people. The tradition of Calvinist republicanism, in which power is deployed, by the providence of God, through the duly appointed representatives of the whole people rather than through a divinely appointed absolute monarch, is in continuity with this. The adoption of 'human rights' thinking, and the enactment of a law protecting human rights, is a *de facto* recognition of a form of 'natural law' since 'human rights' as such are heuristically derived from nothing other than our common humanity.

The specific rights and duties enumerated in the Human Rights Act are, of course, controversial. The practical reasoning by which Christians arrive at an understanding of, say, the 'right to life' will be different to that of non-Christians because it must be accountable to the witness of Scripture. There will be genuine debate between Christians and non-Christians, and among Christians, about the relation between a 'right to life' and the parameters within which abortion might be allowed, or between the 'right to a fair trial' and the right to trial before a jury. There may be sharply different understandings of, say, the right to marry, or the right to found a family: the point is that at the transcendental level, the level of the conditions for social interaction that is not dysfunctional, a series of foundational ('natural') principles have been spelt out and enacted in law. There will rightly be theological and philosophical debate about how to move from a broad understanding of the foundation of 'human rights' in natural law to specific social policies, but Christians need have no hesitation about developing the theological grounds for positive engagement in such public debates.

Alasdair MacIntyre has shown very well how different understandings of natural law will go with different understandings of justice and different understandings of practical rationality. He has also shown how the link between an understanding of natural law and an Aristotelian style of practical reasoning was broken in the eighteenth century. My suggestion here is that it was not the demise of normative Aristotelianism as such which was theologically damaging, but the loss of belief in natural law as a foundation for public, moral rationality which it took with it. At a deep level, the foundation for a positive, Christian social theology was knocked away. I have further suggested that Christians should now take courage from the implicit postulation of 'natural law' in the Human Rights Act, albeit in secular form. Just as the universalist, deist tradition of 'natural law' thinking in Stoicism was critically incorporated into Christian theology in the early years of the church, so the universalist, secular tradition of human-rights thinking can act as a stimulus to Christian social theology today. The key (and the challenge) is a recovery of confidence in 'natural law'. What it has not been possible to cover in one short chapter is a deeper investigation into the ways in which thinkers like Finnis, Nussbaum, Sen and MacIntyre are probing, by their 'thick' description of human flourishing, new forms of natural-law thinking. How they might be drawn upon in a creative social theology based on 'natural law', and in the service of 'God's justice', would be material for another chapter.

Notes

1. Cf. H. R. Niebuhr, *Christ and Culture*, London: Faber, 1952, pp. 58–92.
2. *Larger Catechism*, Answer to Question 93. See T. F. Torrance, ed., *The School of Faith*, London: James Clarke, 1959, p. 204. The moral law is, in Calvinist thought, an aspect of

'common grace', due to which fallen human beings retain
by God's grace a 'consciousness of the difference between
right and wrong, truth and falsehood, justice and injustice,
and the awareness that [they are] answerable or accountable
not merely to [their] fellowmen, but also ultimately to God'.
See Hughes's article on 'Grace' in W. A. Elwell, ed.,
Evangelical Dictionary of Theology, Carlisle: Paternoster,
1984, p. 480.

3. A. MacIntyre, *Whose Justice? Which Rationality?*, London:
Duckworth, 1988, pp. 285, 301 (my emphasis).

4. For a workmanlike account, see K. Haakonssen, *Natural
Law and Moral Philosophy*, Cambridge: Cambridge
University Press, 1996, pp. 182–265.

5. See S. J. Brown, *Thomas Chalmers and the Godly Commonwealth in Scotland*, Oxford: Oxford University Press, 1982.

6. J. Finnis, *Natural Law and Natural Rights*, Oxford:
Clarendon, 1980.

7. For example, 'Aristotelian Social Democracy', in R. B.
Douglass et al., eds, *Liberalism and the Good*, New York:
Routledge, 1990, pp. 203–52.

8. E. Troeltsch argued classically (see *The Social Teaching of
the Christian Churches*, 2 vols, London: SPCK, 1931) that
the incorporation of 'natural law' thinking into Christian
ethics provided a basis for Christian social and political
thought which was lacking in the primitive Gospel, but it
also represented a compromise with pagan thought.
Distinctive of Catholic social teaching was an acceptance of
this compromise; distinctive of Protestant social thinking was
its rejection. This over-simple distinction is much more
representative of a Lutheran approach to 'law and Gospel'
than a Calvinist approach to nature and grace.

9. *De Resp.*, III. xxii. 33–4.

10. Marcus Aurelius, *Meditations*, edited by M. Staniforth,
Harmondsworth: Penguin, 1964, II.9, p. 47.

11. *On the Statutes*, 12.3.

12. *De Lib. Arb.*, I.6.

13. Ibid., I.8.

14. *S.T.* 1a 2ae 90.4, resp. 1.

15. *S.T.* 1a 2ae 91.2, resp.

16. See the detailed note in J. T. McNeil, ed., *Calvin: Institutes
of the Christian Religion*, Library of Christian Classics Series,
vols XX and XXI, Philadelphia: The Westminster Press,

1960, vol. 1, pp. 367–8, commenting on *Inst.* 2.8.1. At the time of the Barthian zenith, McNeil wrote: 'The assumption of some contemporary theologians that natural law has no place in the company of Reformation theology cannot be allowed to govern historical enquiry or lead us to ignore, minimize, or evacuate of reality, the positive utterances on natural law scattered through the works of the Reformers.' See 'Natural law in the teaching of the reformers', *Journal of Religion* 26 (1946), p. 168.

17. *Inst.* 2.2.13, my emphasis.

18. MacIntyre, *Whose Justice?*, p. 226.

19. Sir James Dalrymple of Stair, *The Institutions of the Laws of Scotland*, Edinburgh: Anderson, 1681, p. 17.

20. Ibid., p. 3.

21. Ibid., p. 4.

22. MacIntyre, *Whose Justice?*, p. 239.

23. F. Hutcheson, *A System of Moral Philosophy*, 2 vols, London: Millar, 1755, p. 1. In this edition, a subscription list is given, the only subscriber to buy two sets being 'Mr Adam Smith, Professor of Moral Philosophy in the University of Glasgow'.

24. Ibid., pp. 268–9.

25. Adam Smith, *The Theory of Moral Sentiments*, edited by D. D. Raphael and A. L. Macfie, Oxford: Clarendon, 1976.

26. In his immensely popular *The Spirit of the Laws* (1748), Montesquieu drew out the elements of variety in known human legal systems, and the tensions between the 'goods' they upheld.

27. A. Skinner, Introduction to *The Wealth of Nations I–III*, London: Penguin, 1999, p. 3.

28. MacIntyre, *Whose Justice?*, p. 281.

29. The Church of Scotland Committee on Church and Nation, Report to the General Assembly 2000, p. 34.

30. In *The Wealth of Nations* (1776), Smith does not pursue the discussion of justice in which he engaged in his *Lectures on Jurisprudence*. Nevertheless, he maintains a strong sense of the social imperative which determines what are intolerable levels of poverty. He discusses the physical and social necessities of which people ought not to be deprived by excessive taxation: 'By necessaries I understand not only the commodities which are indispensibly necessary for the support of life, but whatever the custom of the country renders it indecent for creditable people, even of the lowest order, to be without'

(A. Smith, *The Wealth of Nations*, Books IV–V, ed. A. Skinner, London: Penguin, 1999, p. 465).

31. Universal Declaration of Human Rights (UDHR), Preamble.
32. Ibid., Preamble and Article 1.
33. F. Klug, *Values for a Godless Age*, London: Penguin, 2000, p. 20.
34. Ibid., pp. 25–6.
35. *Pacem in Terris, Acta Apostolicae Sedis* 55, 1963, p. 264.
36. Catholic Bishops' Conference of England and Wales, *Human Rights and the Catholic Church*, London: Catholic Media Office, 1998, p. 4.
37. T. F. Torrance makes the case for a 'deeper and more dynamic concept of *natural law*' to act as the foundation of juridical law in *Juridical Law and Physical Law: Towards a Realist Foundation for Human Law*, Edinburgh: Scottish Academic Press, 1982, p. xi. He argues that 'In Britain … legal positivism has been built into the Constitution itself, so that if there is to be an advance towards a realist foundation for our law, the Constitution must be changed. The primary fact that needs to be altered is the investing of Parliament or rather the House of Commons with absolute Sovereignty, and the cognate fact that all law is ultimately reduced to statute law' (p. 18). He adds the rider: 'However, this is now modified by UK adherence to … the European Convention on Human Rights' (p. 19). While I do not share Torrance's confidence in the 'realism' of physical law as an analogy for a 'realist' ontology of moral law, I think the incisiveness of his remarks linking the implementation of the European Convention on Human Rights at 'a third level of law-making' (p. 13) to a renewed understanding of natural law is remarkable.

[Sir Walter] Scott's art was to conceal the psychic tensions between the recording of progress and the politics of reaction. Throughout the 19th and into the 20th century the compromise he brokered allowed Scots to have their bannock and eat it too. They could enjoy the fruits of the empire without either sacrificing their mythic past or letting any disruptive political genies out of the bottle. Under the long hegemony of ethical liberalism, Scottish politics took on an other-worldly air, debating how best to construct the godly commonwealth of Knox and Chalmers in an unregenerate world. Since everyone knew none of these plans would ever negotiate the rapids of Westminister, politics entered the realm of make-believe. Materially, this state of suspended animation did Scotland no harm. Individually, many Scots did well out of the Empire. Being psychologically thirled to a progressive British Whig ideology was probably a positive advantage. The counterbalancing costs kicked in on the cultural, moral and spiritual side. As individuals Scots might be held responsible for their actions – Calvinism is very hot on individual responsibility. But as a group the Scots were precluded from any kind of political intervention and as a result they lapsed into a kind of detached *accidie*. In this light the establishment of the new Parliament opens up an opportunity for Scotland to re-enter political time, restarting the clock that stopped in 1707 and to resume collective responsibility for its own future. One step would be to create a virile post-Ossian Gaelic culture asserting its own vision in the face of the world. Another would be to recognise the real complexities and ambiguities of Scotland – ethnic, linguistic, geographical, etc. – against the facile stereotypes.

Dennis Smith, 'Proposals for a new
Scottish parliament', in *Without Day*

4

The Political Service
of Theology in Scotland

Duncan B. Forrester

I start with two parables which seem to me to illustrate
aptly some of the emphases which we try to express in
the work of the Centre for Theology and Public Issues.

Two Parables

The first comes from the wonderful morality play by Sir
David Lindsay, *Ane Satyre of the Thrie Estaitis*, which
was first performed at the Palace of Linlithgow before
Mary Queen of Scots and her court in 1540, early in the
disturbances which led to the Scottish Reformation. It
was sensationally revived at the first Edinburgh International Festival, and has been performed many times
since then.

At the climax of the play, Poor John the Commonweal
moves centre stage for the first time. His voice has been
but rarely heard until this point in the drama. Now it
comes loud and clear from the heart of the action. Poor
John is supported and encouraged by two other char-
acters. On his right is Divine Correctioun, while on his
left stands Gude Counsel, grasping the book of the
Gospels. Poor John, the ordinary Scot, the one who is
commonly forgotten in high places, whose interests and

feelings are rarely taken into account, now denounces the oppression and the injustice, the self-obsession and the arrogance of each of the 'thrie estaitis' in turn – the burgesses or merchants, the nobility and the church. John calls for justice and for peace, for a purification of church and state, for a society that is fair and decent and gives priority to the interests of the weak and the poor and the forgotten.

Poor John's speech to the powerful, his call to them to do justice and love mercy and walk humbly with their God, became a central concern of the Scottish Reformation. Alongside purity of doctrine and worship, the establishment of justice, the ending of oppression, and what would today be called a 'preferential option for the poor', were central concerns in the early Reformation period. Church courts, according to *The First Book of Discipline*, were concerned with charges of 'oppressing of the poore by exactions', and 'deceiving of them in buying and selling by wrang met and measure'. Knox himself taught that 'the dear commonalty of Scotland' were responsible to God for the behaviour of their rulers, and ought to demand justice and fair dealing from them, as Poor John the Commonweal had done.

Here, surely, is a great heritage, and a mandate for speaking truth to power!

My second parable comes from more recent times, from Czechoslovakia before the collapse of the communist regimes of Eastern Europe. It is told almost as a coded piece of autobiography by Václav Havel, former dissident and now President of the Czech Republic, in a remarkable book entitled, significantly, *Living in Truth*.[1]

Havel tells the parable of a greengrocer during the days of the communist dictatorship, who one week puts in his window, among the carrots and tomatoes, the slogan 'Workers of the World Unite!', and the next week 'Struggle Together for World Peace!' Why does he do it?

- Because the slogan has been delivered to him from the wholesalers along with the fruit and vegetables;
- Because everyone else does it;
- Because he has done this sort of thing for years;
- Because if he refused there would be trouble; he would be accused of disloyalty;
- Because this harmless action ensures a tranquil life for him.

The greengrocer is not very interested in what the slogans *say*. He certainly does not feel he is communicating some exciting new truth to his customers. The reflex action, week by week, of putting up the slogan in his window simply means: 'I am dependable and obedient, and I want to be left in peace.'

The words of the slogans in the greengrocer's window, Havel suggests, not only conceal the degradation of his condition, but they also hide the realities of the system behind a façade of respectability, morality and high aspirations. They suggest that the system is in harmony with the moral order, that power and truth are at one.

But that is not true. The greengrocer is living in a lie. And most of the time his life is more comfortable that way.

Now, suppose that one day something snaps in our greengrocer. He refuses any longer to put up slogans so that he can have a quiet life. He starts to speak his mind in public. He seeks out and befriends other dissidents. He no longer plays by the rules of the game. He steps out of living in the lie. He begins to live in the truth.

His bill is not long in coming. He loses his job. Old friends shun him in the street. His children can't get places in college. He has to move house and take a job sweeping the streets.

His little dissent radically shakes the assumption that truth and power are one. His tiny protest is an earth-quake: what is foolish in the world has shamed the wise, what is weak in the world has shamed the strong. The powerless find power when they live in truth. They live not in truth in isolation but together, in solidarity. The very notion of living in truth is inescapably concerned with others. This community is responsible for the world and for those who are not its members. It cannot be introverted, *incurvatus in se*, concerned only for itself.

Christians also believe that the truth is something to be lived and loved within the fellowship of the church and reaching forward to the coming Reign of God. It is not just a matter of thought, of systems of ideas, of propositions. The truths that emerge from the endeavour to live in truth are usually in fragments, hints, clues, cries, questions, pointers. These are the 'puzzling reflections in a mirror' of which 1 Corinthians 13 speaks. This truth cannot be manipulated, comprehended or controlled; nor is it oppressive and coercive as most grand systems are. This truth can only be loved, and lived in, and reverenced, and worshipped. And only at the end will the dimness and distortion of the mirror be replaced with a face-to-face personal encounter with the truth.

Havel's greengrocer reminds us of the imperative to speak truth to power, and of the dangers of sloganising rather than offering serious and rigorous theology. It reminds us that theological truth is something to be lived, to be exemplified, rather than just thought and discussed; it is to be lived *together* in the life of the church and in society. And it is a truth that is concrete, challenging and specific rather than general and platitudinous.

The Political Service of Theology

Karl Barth, probably the greatest theologian of the twentieth century, affirmed frequently that all theology was implicitly or explicitly political, and that theology was never detached discourse about a reality that did not impinge on the life of the world, but was always relevant to the needs and suffering and hopes of people and communities in what is often called 'the real world'. Theology has a service to make in and to the political sphere, while recognising and affirming the distinct and important mandate of the state. But theology, Barth taught, cannot serve the world truthfully by diluting itself, or by disguising itself as something different. Indeed, true theology is doxology, the praise of God, and confession, public witnessing to God's truth, a truth which comes to us but cannot be grasped, comprehended or domesticated. The faith is confessed and God is served in particular contexts in particular ways. That is why Christians have to learn how to 'discern the signs of the times', and consider what God is calling them to do in a particular place and at a particular time.

When Barth came to Aberdeen to deliver the Gifford Lectures in the particular context of 1937 and 1938 – Nazism seemed all-powerful, and a cataclysmic war loomed ahead – he spoke of *The Knowledge of God and the Service of God*.[2] He stressed that the life and worship of the church always had huge implications for the life of the world, and that the state also was called to the service of God, from whom it received its mandate. Knowledge of God, Barth argued, is inseparable from the service of God. 'Knowledge of God according to the

teaching of the Reformation', he argued, 'is *obedience*
to God and therefore itself already service of God . . .
Knowledge of God is nothing other than service of God.'[3]
By 'service', Barth means both worship and practical
obedience to God. Theology in this understanding is not
a free-floating academic discipline developed on the basis
of reason rather than revelation, the same everywhere
and always. It is inseparably tied to Christian faith. It
has at its heart christology, the understanding of the
person and the call of Jesus Christ. And it addresses particular issues and contexts in quite specific and concrete
ways.

  This is part of Barth's sustained attack on what he
called 'natural theology' – rational reflection on the being
and calling of God. Natural theology, Barth believed,
while claiming to be universal, acts like blotting paper: it
sucks up the assumptions and prejudices of the day, and
is incapable of exercising a proper critique of the spirit
of the age. The liberal version of natural theology, he
argued, had shown its ineffectiveness and shallowness,
its inability to do more than reflect the assumptions of
the time, with the outbreak of the First World War, and
its enthusiastic endorsement by liberal theologians on both
sides; later forms of natural theology, he argued, had
proved themselves powerless in face of the rise of Nazism.

  In 1941, when many responsible and intelligent
observers believed that victory against Hitler was
impossible, Barth sent *A Letter to Great Britain from
Switzerland* which was a direct call to arms against
Nazism: 'The Christians who do not realise that they
must take part unreservedly in this war must have slept
over their Bibles as well as over their newspapers', he
wrote.[4] His argument in this tract was, he claimed,
founded not on the rational approach of natural law or
natural theology, but rather 'the ultimate reason which

I put forward for the necessity of resisting Hitler was simply the resurrection of Jesus Christ'.⁵ And much of the letter was spent in arguing for the necessity of a social theology which was an expression of the central truths of the Christian faith rather than an afterthought or an appendix, or simply a theological blessing on conclusions reached for quite other reasons. 'All arguments based on natural law', he argued, 'are Janus-headed. They do not lead to the light of clear decisions, but to the misty reality in which all cats become grey. They lead – to Munich.'⁶ Social and political theology, if it is to be clear, useful, faithful and enlightening, must be unashamedly theological. That, according to Karl Barth, is the distinctive Christian gift and service in the public realm. For theology is an engagement with the living God.

The Relevance of the Radical Scottish Tradition

Rather to the surprise of many people in Scotland, Barth chose to frame his 1938 Gifford Lectures, which in one sense were wrestling with the concrete issues of the German Church Struggle and the growing power of Nazism, and in another way engaging with perennial issues of theology and life, around a then almost forgotten document from the Reformation period, the *Scots Confession* of 1560. The reasons for this are not hard to seek. Barth found the *Scots Confession* christological through and through. Unlike the later *Westminster Confession*, the *Scots Confession* does not speak of a natural theology complementing revealed theology. It eschews rational or scholastic theology. The times demand clear and unambiguous Christian confession, and a call to active obedience. And this call to obedience is uncompromising.

The *Scots Confession* is among the most radical Reformation documents, delimiting strictly the powers of the ruler, distinguishing church and state without neglecting their responsibilities to one another, and actually affirming a right, indeed a duty, of resistance to unjust rule. The *Scots Confession* teaches that human nature since the Fall is fundamentally flawed; nature is fallen and corrupt; there is no way to God other than by faith and grace; by nature human beings are incapable of serving or knowing God. Barth saw the *Scots Confession* as anticipating his own rejection of natural theology.

At the time of the delivery of the Gifford Lectures, few Scottish theologians were interested in, or knowledgeable about, the *Scots Confession*; it would seem that the radical tradition represented by the *Scots Confession*, and the *First Book of Discipline* produced in the same year, 1560, was no longer lively in Scotland.[7] Barth's excitement at discovering the *Scots Confession* might serve as an encouragement to us, in discussing the service that social theology might render in Scotland today, to turn to the past of theological involvement in public life in Scotland, expecting to find there guidance and encouragement, and also warnings of the damage that can be caused when things go wrong.

From the sixteenth century, Scotland has maintained a somewhat distinctive understanding of the relationship of church and state, church and society. The ruler has not been recognised as 'Supreme Governor' of the church, as in England, or as *primus episcopus*, as in many of the Lutheran lands of the continent of Europe. The ruler should be a member of the church, and has responsibilities towards the church. Andrew Melville, the leader of the Second Reformation, who in an encounter with James VI at Falkland in 1596 called the king 'bot God's sillie vassall', typified the early relationship between church and state. Melville sees his task at a time of crisis for church and Crown to speak truth to power and clarify what he sees as the true Reformed relationship of church and state. Here is a strong affirmation of the sole Lordship of Christ, which relativises all earthly sovereignties, and a powerful suggestion that this is mediated to the civil authorities by the Kirk, which in a special sense is the Kingdom of Christ. This distinctively Scottish version of the 'two kingdoms' theory may from time to time have been open to the opposite dangers to those latent in the Anglican Reformation's affirmation of the royal supremacy.[8] It certainly involved a claim on the part of the church to spiritual independence, which was seen by royalists in the sixteenth and seventeenth centuries as an unacceptable limitation on royal power, and which could easily become theocracy, or even the unqualified power of ministers.

The Scots Reformed tradition also stresses peculiarly strongly the responsibilities laid upon ordinary people. They were responsible to God for their government's actions, and shared with government responsibility for establishing justice and opposing tyranny and oppression. The resistance to a tyrant which was grudgingly conceded by Luther and Calvin, under strictly defined conditions, in the *Scots Confession* became a duty.

The Scots Reformed tradition of social theology is thus, as I have tried very briefly to show, strongly confessional and biblical. It stresses that the church and the state are distinct communities that have reciprocal responsibilities. All power flows from God, and human beings are responsible to God for the way they exercise this power. The community as a whole is in a covenantal relationship with God; its whole life is to be lived towards God. But the church is not simply the one united community viewed from a different angle, with all citizens being regarded as disciples and all disciples as citizens, and usually with the monarch as the common head of church and state. Although the nations might be a covenanted community, the church was a sign and a challenge to the whole community because it was an anticipation and a kind of working model of God's coming Reign.

A Living Tradition

The radical strand in the Scottish tradition of social theology has always emphasised the necessity for theology and the church to offer a distinctive and strongly biblical and confessional contribution to public life. It still shows itself today in a sometimes quite obsessive determination in the Church of Scotland to ground its public statements in the Bible. At its best, this results in the church making a recognised and significant contribution to public debate, as did the Church and Nation Committee's 1989 report on the Constitution which demonstrated with great clarity that there was a distinct and democratic Scottish tradition of thought on sovereignty and the constitution which was grounded in theology and widely recognised as highly relevant to the developing debate on devolution and the reform of the constitution. Another example might be the report of a Church and Nation working party on the distribution of wealth, income and benefits, published as *Just Sharing* in 1988.[9] This book attempted to ground its work in theological and biblical reflection, and saw this as its distinctive service in this area. *Just Sharing* was presented to Mrs Thatcher by the Moderator at the conclusion of her famous 'Sermon on the Mound' in 1988 as a kind of challenge to Thatcherite orthodoxy.

The contrast with the Church of Scotland's contribution to the 1969 Crowther-Kilbrandon Commission on the constitution is marked. At that time, the church's representatives disavowed any competence or distinctive insights in matters constitutional, and argued that they came to the Commission simply as representatives of a major element of Scottish public opinion, and as concerned for the future good of Scotland. They spoke in effect as claiming to represent the opinions of many Scots, rather than as people confessing the Christian faith in relation to a specific nation, moment and area of debate. And yet it must also be admitted that biblical and theological arguments in church reports are often wooden, literalist and unimaginative; such arguments cannot find a point of entry into the general public debate.

There is that in the tradition of social theology that I have sketched which is no longer relevant in a pluralistic, secular age.[10] And there are distinctive dangers in the tradition which still require to be addressed. But we have also seen developments in the last fifty years or so which suggest that it may have continuing vitality and relevance in these days. For example, the Theological Declaration of Barmen of 1934 was an immensely influential confessional statement against Hitler and Nazism, and the struggle against apartheid in South Africa had close to its heart arguments about biblical interpretation, a series of confessional statements, and the ecumenical declarations that apartheid was a confessional issue of such gravity that those Christians who defended apartheid should be excluded from the fellowship of the church. The critique of natural law developed by Barth and discerned by him as already there in the early documents of the Scottish Reformation apparently retains its saliency. Nature, as we observe and experience it, is according to Reformed theology fallen, a broken remnant of God's original order and final purpose. God's purposes, being and commands cannot now be read off nature as we find it. Natural theology easily reflects back the conventional wisdom of the age – but biblical and confessional arguments, too, may be used to buttress prejudices or conceal interests.

The Scottish Reformation had a strong conviction that reformation involved not just doctrine, worship and the life of the church, but that the whole of society should be reformed. The *Scots Confession* itself said many things about the responsibilities of rulers and of subjects; it was complemented by *The First Book of Discipline* of 1560, which not only outlined the reconstruction of the Kirk that was required but outlined a programme by which the whole life of the community and the nation was to be shaped in accordance with God's commands and should reflect the divine purpose of justice and love.[11] This broad concern was expressed down the ages in the church's involvement in education, poor relief and social justice as well as individual behaviour, with the commitment to what Thomas Chalmers in the nineteenth century called 'the Christian good of Scotland'. And the concern encompasses far more than Scotland. In more recent times, this surfaced, for example, in the General Assembly's immensely influential Special Commission on Central Africa, and in the ongoing work of the Church and Nation Committee and of the Board of Social Responsibility. The Special Commission on Central Africa, led by George MacLeod, played a significant role in the dismantling of the Central African Federation. In 1959, the General Assembly responded enthusiastically to MacLeod's call to support the opposition to the Central African Federation: 'Someone must speak for the Africans, and that someone will be the General Assembly of the Church of Scotland', he said.

Interestingly enough, Roman Catholic social teaching has in recent years moved from an almost sole dependence on natural-law reasoning to a far greater reliance on Scripture and serious and sustained endeavours to discern what God is doing in our times, and calling us to do. This is perhaps most marked in John Paul II's encyclical *Centesimus Annus* (1991), but it is a general development in the wake of the Second Vatican Council. That encyclical not only celebrates the centenary of *Rerum Novarum* but very seriously asks what God is doing and saying in 'the New Things of Today', and especially seeks to interpret theologically the momentous events of 'The Year 1989'. Thus today a shared commitment to the serious task of discerning the signs of the times together with a joint conviction of the centrality of Scripture brings together Christians from various traditions in the development of a social theology responsive to the needs, problems and opportunities of today.

The Scottish tradition of social theology is, I believe, largely confessional and evangelical. It has a gospel to share, good news to proclaim. It attends to the Bible and the tradition of faith at the same time as it attempts to discern the signs of the times and understand what is going on in the light of the Gospel. Since the seventeenth century, this has often been linked to a classical or Enlightenment form of natural theology, as in Samuel Rutherford or Thomas Chalmers. I have tried to show, in relation to Chalmers, that his reliance on natural theology in his social thinking in relation to poverty encouraged an account of poverty and attitudes towards poor people which were sharply at variance with the gospel.[12] In the pluralist, fragmented and secular society of today, the question of natural theology is raised with a new urgency, as the only way of uniting believers and others in pursuit of a common good which is understood as unrelated to religious specifics and the understanding of which is accessible to everyone. While there is much in these efforts to forge a consensus around shared ideas of the good that is attractive and valuable, there is a danger that public debate may be impoverished by being denied the distinctive truths and insights of Christian faith. It is not only in times of crisis, such as the rise of Nazism or the struggle against apartheid, that a confessional approach has much to commend itself, even in a plural society. It is by turns a challenge, a corrective or a complement to approaches which are in some way or another based on natural theology.

Discernment[13]

The kind of public theology that I am exploring is very much concerned with discerning what God is doing in the events of today, and what God is calling us to do. But what do we mean by 'discernment' of the signs of the times? The signs of the times discussed in the gospels[14] are manifestations of a new order latent in the disorder of the day, ready to emerge from the womb of the past. The scribes and Pharisees wanted a sign authenticating Jesus and the message of God's Reign which he preached. They wanted all doubt removed. They sought certainty before they decided how to respond. They were not willing to take a risk. They wanted a sign so that they could be sure beyond a shadow of a doubt that the Jesus movement was the manifestation of God's Reign before they responded to Jesus, before they *did* anything, before they joined the new community, before they committed themselves. They wanted proof, certainty, before they decided how to respond to this strange, compelling teacher and his call to discipleship.

And, in the narrative, those who seek for a sign at the beginning, before they chance their arm, before they respond to the needs and sufferings of the world, are condemned by Jesus as an evil and adulterous generation. This generation is on the make, looking after its own interests, putting number one first, for its affections are free-floating and unattached. It cries out in a childish way for certainty where no certainty is to be had. It calls for a sign. But the true sign is the new order growing secretly in the midst of the chaos and violence of the world, a reality which is only to be discerned by faith, not by formula.

Strangely and ominously, the gospel narratives stress that the scribes and Pharisees, for all their inherited Scriptural wisdom and knowledge of God's people's experience of God's activity in history, were unable to read the signs of the times. The signs require a different sort of discernment from that of the scribes and Pharisees. It is not easy, perhaps, for intellectuals, for people of status and position, to discern that the emperor has no clothes on, and that a new and different order, the Reign of God, is breaking in.

How then do we discern the signs of the times? Discernment is certainly not a mechanical process, the application of simple clues or principles or guidelines from Scripture or from elsewhere. Intellectuals and theologians and ecclesiastics probably have special diffi-culties in discernment, because they have so often lost simplicity of vision and fallen into the grip of systems or ideologies which conceal at least as much as they reveal, so that they are not open to the radically new. To discern, we need to recover true simplicity. Discernment means putting the events and choices and responses of today within the frame of eternity, taking the long view, with attitudes and understanding shaped by faith and imbued with hope.

And such discernment can lead to new and challenging insights in the public realm, and provide the context in which we may hear God's call. It can also lead to a rejection of the conventional wisdom and the dominant priorities in the public sphere. In 1933, when the German Christians and many others were seeing Hitler's coming to power as a turning point in history, virtually the climax of salvation history, Karl Barth decided that the most effective counter to this heresy was just to continue to explore the implications of the true turning point of history, to witness to the truth of God by doing as rigorous theology as possible:

> Here, with my students in lectures and courses, I endeavour to carry on theology, and only theology, now as previously, and as if nothing had happened. Perhaps there is a slightly increased tone, but without direct allusions: something like the chanting of the hours by the Benedictines near by in the *Maria Laach*, which goes on undoubtedly without break or interruption, pursuing the even tenor of its way even in the *Third Reich*. I regard the pursuit of theology as the proper attitude to adopt: at any rate it is one befitting church-politics, and, indirectly, even politics.[15]

This is not escaping from the problems of today, but engaging with them at a deeper level.

Speak Out for Those who Cannot Speak

Liberation theologians characteristically see a central part of their role as standing with and speaking for the poor and the excluded, the ones who are commonly without a voice, fulfilling the biblical injunction:

> Speak out for those who cannot speak,
> for the rights of all the destitute.
> Speak out, judge righteously,
> defend the rights of the poor and needy.[16]

The liberation theologians, I believe, are right in affirming this role of the theologians, to speak for the poor and weak and the voiceless. Only those who stand with those who are denied a voice can articulate their voice and contribute thus to the search for truth, not allowing the meanings of the powerful and intellectual to dominate the discussion and exclude or despise other voices. A proper objectivity is often compatible with taking sides; indeed taking sides, commitment, can be an avenue to truth. The liberation theologians' insight at this point is of broad relevance and importance.

It is, I believe, bad in principle and bad in practice to talk about people behind their backs, particularly if they are relatively powerless people who are often labelled 'problems', and one is talking about their problems and how to solve them.

In social theology, there is a need to put scientific study of the situation at the service of a more affective or emotional approach[17] which enables us to see things through others' eyes and leads to a more adequate and rounded understanding of the situation. I am trying to avoid using words like 'sympathy' or 'compassion' because they have been so devalued in common usage. But they both in origin mean feeling together, putting oneself in the other person's shoes and sharing at the level of feeling in order to deepen the understanding and strengthen the will to do something to improve the situation. And this is precisely what I am talking about.

An Experiment in Public Theology

The Centre for Theology and Public Issues in the University of Edinburgh was initially established to attempt to meet a widely expressed need for a serious Christian think-tank in Scotland on social, constitutional

and political issues which could act as a resource for the
churches and others in contributing to public debate. It
should be ecumenical and seek academic rigour in all its
work. It was to engage with specific issues, where people
are hurting, where there is much uncertainty, and often
where serious communication among those of differing
commitments, experiences and views has more or less
broken down. The Centre was to try to predict and
engage with the issues that would be on the public
agenda tomorrow, or next year, rather than with the
issues that everyone was talking about and studying at
the present moment. This forward look was to ensure
that we did not simply repeat what everyone was saying
anyway, or duplicate research that was going on
elsewhere. Instead, we were to try to equip the churches
and theologians to prepare seriously for tomorrow's
debates.

CTPI was intended to be, and from the beginning was
in fact, a thoroughly interdisciplinary operation,
involving people from many different specialities and
various kinds of experience in its work. It had, and has,
a special care for the place of theology. This is a remarkably tricky matter, partly as a result of academic speciali-
sation which has pushed much theology into cultivating
what is considered its own cabbage patch, and seldom
looking over the garden fence, let alone talking with the
neighbours. Occasionally, we succeeded in CTPI in
offering theological insights that were regarded as
strikingly relevant; but sometimes the theology didn't
connect. Increasingly, we discovered that people became
involved in our work because we provided a highly
unusual kind of forum, and they were anxious, even if
they had no Christian commitment, to hear whether
theology had anything relevant and interesting to say.
There are many people in academic and public life who

embrace Christian attitudes and values, and whose lives often put us card-carrying Christians to shame, people who want to know about the roots of the values they know to be true, and want to know if Christianity makes a difference.

We also had in the work of CTPI from very early on a determination not to speak about people and their problems behind their backs. It was important to embrace and understand the human reality of social problems, to share feelings and emotions as well as thoughts and ideas. So when we are discussing poverty, we have poor people as full participants; when we are talking about homelessness, there are homeless people present. This often has interesting and important results. I remember occasions when, after extremely fine and humane presentations by leading scholars, a poor or homeless person has got up and shouted angrily: 'You don't know what you are talking about!' In a very important sense, that cry is true. Some academics and some theologians turn away from such angry, inarticulate and confusing debate to more orderly academic discourse. But others see attending to such voices as a very central part of engaging *together* with the hurts and the pain that many people are suffering. Then, and only then, there sometimes comes the time when there is a responsibility of speaking for those who have no voice.

Sometimes the motivation for a sustained study comes from experience of a situation where communication has broken down, where people are speaking past one another rather than attending to what others have to say. For example, some years ago we had a conference on finance and ethics. The input was of a high quality, but it quickly became clear that there was no communication between those who had great responsibilities in the Scottish financial world, and tended to be very cautious in their public utterances, and the critics, who saw no way forward other than the dismantling of the financial system and its replacement by something which is totally different and morally entirely unobjectionable. Gathering a mixed group from all sides of the question and arranging for them to meet in private sessions under 'Chatham House rules' gradually led to a different and more productive kind of discourse. The leading financiers were able in such a context to admit that they sometimes had doubts about the moral acceptability of processes and decisions in which they were involved; the critics came to see that they needed to talk of change, reform and improvement rather than simply challenge and confrontation. As the members of the group gained confidence in one another, they decided that they should stay together, so they formed a Finance and Ethics Network, which met until recently and they began publishing a *Finance and Ethics Quarterly*.

I will now say a little about three projects which attempted to embody these principles. In 1984, we were asked by the Church and Nation Committee of the Church of Scotland to undertake a study of the distribution of wealth, income and benefits. A working group was established, composed of people with a wide range of experience and expertise. It met regularly for more than two years, and received opinions, advice and information from a wide variety of sources. A brief report was presented to the General Assembly of the Church of Scotland in 1987, and congregations and Kirk Sessions were encouraged to discuss these matters further. The fuller version of the report was published as a book, *Just Sharing: A Christian Approach to the Distribution of Wealth, Income and Benefits* in 1987.[18] This book was presented by the Moderator to the then Prime Minister, Margaret Thatcher, when she visited the

General Assembly to deliver her 'Sermon on the Mound'. It was also discussed widely in churches and community groups, and with politicians and academics.

The first task of the group was to face the facts and to discover something of what these facts mean in human terms for individuals, for families and for the nation. We then moved on to reflection and interpretation, looking to the Bible and the Christian tradition for clues, insights, signals and challenges. Finally, we discussed how we should respond to what we had found – theologically, the question of how we should respond to Jesus Christ and the neighbours he has given us today. We felt that to be serious we had to respond on three fronts simultaneously, looking at issues of personal life-style, then at the life of the church, and only then at questions of public policy.

None of the working group were themselves poor, although we attended to the voices of poor people. We all had a kind of security which meant that we had never experienced from the inside the powerlessness and vulnerability of the poor. We had not had our children going hungry to bed, been unable to make ends meet, or felt politically impotent. But some of us had been challenged deeply by involvement in situations of great poverty and inequality. Some of us had had our understanding of ourselves, of our faith, and of how we should lead our lives fundamentally transformed by finding ourselves implicated in situations of poverty and maldistribution. We listened to poor people, and one of the things we heard from a woman in Easterhouse, a deprived area of eastern Glasgow, was this: 'The church should be teaching people about God. So everything's its business.'

And it wasn't only the working group that listened. As part of the 'reception' of *Just Sharing*, much unusual and significant listening took place. I remember well a conference in a deprived council estate, organised by local community groups, political parties and churches, to which we were invited essentially to listen. I was asked by a group of wealthy and influential businessmen if they could attend. After consultation with the conference organisers, I said yes, on two conditions – that a small number of them came so as not to swamp the conference, and that they devoted their time to listening rather than talking. I spent much of the afternoon in a small group with one of the most powerful businessmen in the city, as local women spoke of the dampness and bad design of many of their homes, the poor medical services in the area, the problems at the schools, the inadequacy of the public transport, and how they were coping with a pervasive drug problem and insensitive policing. The businessman had never heard this kind of thing before. It was a learning experience for him.

Another area in which we have done work is prisons and punishment.[19] It all started with a conference in the course of which it became clear that the Scottish prison system, and much of the criminal justice system, was in a state of disarray, and this confusion was deeply harmful to society. We set up an interdisciplinary working group, with prison governors, chaplains and educational officers, with a couple of bright young criminologists, with theologians and with a minister of the Church of Scotland who had been in prison for murder. His case was interesting in itself, for there had been, a couple of years before the group was convened, a notable debate in the General Assembly of the Church of Scotland about whether this man and another man who had been imprisoned for embezzlement were eligible to be ordained. The debate polarised around a large minority who argued that the standing of the Christian ministry depended on ministers being above reproach, and a small majority who argued that Christian ministry was about a gospel of grace and forgiveness, and a personal experience of great forgiveness qualified a minister to speak of grace from his own experience. A friend of mine who was a prison chaplain told me that, when he was on his rounds not long after this debate, he found a prisoner in tears. He told the chaplain that he had been an elder, and his wife had visited him and told him that last Sunday for the first time since his conviction she had felt able to go to church, as she now realised that the church really believed in the forgiveness of sins.

The turning point in the working group's deliberations was this. After a long and depressing (because so unrelated to what actually went on in prisons) look at the current theories of punishment – rehabilitation, retribution, deterrence and so forth – a Christian female prison governor said, very quietly: 'There are two things that few people pay much attention to in Scottish prisons these days – guilt, as a process with which individuals have to come to terms, and forgiveness, healing and restoration of community.' This started a very exciting two hours of discussion, at the end of which we all agreed that any system of punishment which was not directed towards the goal of reconciliation, healing and forgiveness was seriously lacking in Christian and moral acceptability. Here we were in fact quarrying into central aspects of the Christian tradition to find help for public policy today.

In this tradition, we found a challenge to the modern assumption that the world is divided neatly and unambiguously into the guilty and the innocent. We are all offenders, standing under the judgment and the grace of God. Consider, for example, this order for the reception back into the congregation of a forgiven offender, coming from the Scots Calvinist tradition, and dating from 1564:

> If we consider his fall and sin in him only, without having consideration of ourselves and of our own corruption, we shall profit nothing, for so shall we but despise our brother and flatter ourselves; but if we shall earnestly consider what nature we bear, what corruption lurketh in it, how prone and ready every one of us is to such and greater impiety, then shall we in the sin of this our brother accuse and condemn our own sins, in his fall we shall consider and lament our sinful nature, also we shall join our repentance, tears and prayers with him and his, knowing that no flesh can be justified before God's presence, if judgment proceed without mercy . . .

> [The minister turns to the penitent and says:]

> You have heard also the affection and care of the church towards you, their penitent brother, notwithstanding your grievous fall, to wit, that we all here present join our sins with your sin; we all repute and esteem your fall to be our own; we accuse ourselves no less than we accuse you; now, finally, we join our prayers with yours, that we and you may obtain mercy, and that by the means of our Lord Jesus Christ.

> [The minister addresses the congregation:]

> Now it only resteth that ye remit and forget all offences which ye have conceived heretofore by the sin and fall of this our brother; accept and embrace him as a member of Christ's body; let no one take upon him to reproach or accuse him for any offences that before this hour he hath committed.[20]

Out of the experience of this project, we found that there was a role for Christian social theology in supporting conscientious and caring people working within the system, often fighting against much discouragement; in influencing public opinion, beginning with the churches, because public opinion is often savage and unforgiving; in constructive suggestions to policy-makers; and in demonstrating that Christian insights may be of importance and relevance in public life today.

My final case is very brief but still, I think, important. On two occasions, in 1987 and in 1998, we have had conferences in which we have brought together a diversity of people from Northern Ireland, from Scotland and from the Republic of Ireland to speak together and to listen on the basis of a shared Christian faith. I remember very vividly at the 1987 conference on *Northern Ireland – A Challenge to Theology*,[21] how Garret Fitzgerald, at that time still Taoiseach of the Republic, and one who has Protestant as well as Roman Catholic roots, honestly outlined his vision for the future, in dialogue with Enda McDonagh and Terry McCaughey. And I remember Enda McDonagh's controversial suggestion that only a clear disjunction between Catholicism and nationalism and Protestantism and unionism will enable Christian faith to survive, and Frank Wright's remarkable discussion of the reconciliation of memories.

And in the 1998 conference on *A Turning Point in Scotland and Ireland? The Challenge to the Churches and Theology Today*,[22] I recall the stress on the similarities between the Scottish and the Irish situation, and the suggestion that we can learn, positively and negatively, from one another. Reconciliation may be a long-drawn-out process, but for Christians it is the recognition and expression of what God has achieved for us in Christ.

And, above all, I remember that saintly Irish Presbyterian theologian, Alan Lewis, who died so tragically young, telling us that we must learn in Scotland and Ireland how to speak the truth to one another in love.

And that, in a real sense, is what we are about in CTPI, learning how to speak truth to power in love and in justice.

Vision[23]

> Write the vision,
> make it plain on tablets,
> so that a runner may read it.
> For there is still a vision for the appointed time;
> it speaks of the end and does not lie.
> If it seems to tarry, wait for it;
> it will surely come; it will not delay.[24]

A serious social theology must be concerned not just with isolated and specific issues – although these are certainly important – but also with vision. This, rather than a grand theory or a splendidly co-ordinated systematic theology, is the broad frame for social theology. Hence vision has been for a number of years a continuing concern of the Centre for Theology and Public Issues.

There is profound truth in the familiar text: 'Where there is no vision the people perish' (Proverbs 29:18). The people perish because without vision they are locked into their past and present and incapable of imagining a future that will be better, because they have lost hope; the horizon of the future has been eroded. Politics in such a situation becomes mere 'business', horse-trading, squabbling about power with little sense of the ends to which power is the means. Gaining and holding onto power become ends in themselves. For vision is what generates purpose for a society. Without vision, public life becomes a battle of interests, unconstrained by a larger horizon of meaning; 'civil war carried on by other means', to use Alasdair MacIntyre's telling phrase, a civil war in which the prizes all go to the victors, and woe to the losers, the powerless and the vulnerable.

A concern with vision serves to remind Christians that theology is not exclusively engaged with 'academic' questions, or with particular problems and policies and ethical conundrums. It is at least as concerned with the visions which provide a horizon of meaning within which a society exists, policies are formulated, actions are taken and vocations are fulfilled. Visions generate and sustain utopias, if you prefer that language. And, as Rubem Alves has suggested, 'When utopias are not imagined, ethics is reduced to solving problems within the established system', and we are at the mercy of an absolutising of a present which is deprived of any eschatological hope. Without vision, people give up seeking a better future, because in the absence of goals social life loses meaning and becomes the arena for unbridled self-interest. A society without vision is petty, selfish and cruel.

Visions have the ability to constrain selfishness and enable altruism, reaching out to the neighbour in love. Visions can open us to God's future and motivate us to seek God's Reign. Visions generate hope and disturb and challenge us, especially when we are comfortable or complacent in the present. Indeed, it is usually people who are weak, marginalised and forgotten, despised people and suffering people who generate visions, who respond to visions, who live by visions.

Not all visions are equally good and desirable, of course. The communist dictatorships in Eastern Europe that collapsed after 1989 reminded us how a vision in some ways admirable could lead to dehumanising dictatorship, and then decay rapidly, eroded by its own inadequacy. And Hitler's dream of the 1,000-year Reich represented a vision that was devastatingly evil. In these recent days of 'tumult and trampling and confusion in the valley of vision' (Isaiah 2:5) there are many visions on offer which are exclusive, petty and even dehumanising. Other visions are simply individual pipe-dreams, ways of escaping from reality rather than engaging with the coming Reign of God. In many situations, as in Northern Ireland, there are powerful polarised and blinkered visions, dominated by bitter and partial memories of the past.

We are in an age when many visions are on offer, and they are often in contention with one another. Different visions compete for people's allegiance. Christians must today learn how to assess visions, how to discriminate between visions. These are great issues from which academics, mainly theologians and social scientists, have to an amazing extent steered clear for many decades, preferring to concentrate on details rather than the broad picture, on description rather than evaluation, on the past and the present rather than God's future. Visions, the kind of visions which generate goals and horizons of meaning, and keep the future open, have been left to 'visionaries', religious people, fanatics. But others too have responsibilities in these matters. At such a time, Christians have a special need to test visions, our own and others. This means that they constantly measure their vision against reality: does it help us to see the world as it is and (even more important, and for Christians, more real) as it might be, more clearly? Does it enable and encourage hopeful, courageous, just and loving behaviour? Does it help us to see evil, oppression, meanness and injustice for what they are, and respond to them with faithful steadfastness?

The term *social* vision has an important inbuilt ambiguity. It can mean a vision of the future of a society, or a vision shared by many or most people in a community. Social vision is necessarily incompatible with the kind of individualism so influential today, and also with the common assumption that the best that can be hoped for is some kind of balance of power. Social vision speaks to us of our interdependence, of our account-ability to one another and our responsibility for one another. It constrains and disciplines individuals and groups in their pursuit of their interests in the light of a higher and more comprehensive good.

Social vision as *shared* vision has peculiar problems in a modern plural society. How can a sectarian vision, or a vision held by a minority, commend itself to a whole great society as something that can generate goals and give cohesion? Imposed visions quickly destroy freedom and become vicious – so much we must have learned since 1945 in Europe. Pluralism can provide goods we would not wish to lose – openness and a degree of freedom for all, for instance. But some contemporary supporters of pluralism commend a thoroughgoing pluralist society which is neither cohesive nor caring, where vision is discounted, perhaps because history is believed to be at an end (Fukuyama), and we have nothing left to hope for.

Modern pluralism thus presents a direct challenge to social vision. For Hayek, as a typical protagonist of pluralism, only small, simple, face-to-face societies are capable of seeking a common goal, of being held together by a shared vision. In large, complex societies, a social vision can only be *imposed*, so that what Hayek calls 'teleocratic' societies are inherently and inescapably dictatorial. The 'great society' that Hayek desires because it provides the conditions for liberty and prosperity is one in which a multitude of individual and group interests are bound loosely together without any over-arching or constraining notion of the common good, or of a shared vision. The operations of an invisible hand to bring about some kind of balance between competing interests and scatter unanticipated goods, or make them 'trickle down', makes some kind of moral sense of the pursuit of individual and specific goals as a poor approximation to a society. It rests on an impoverished idea of community as simply an arena of conflicting interests, where the nearest approximation to justice is some kind of equilibrium and the observance of some simple rules of fair dealing.

The inadequacy of this abandonment of the need for a shared vision and common goals is neatly demonstrated by the present turmoil in three social institutions which, like many, cannot be fully integrated into the market or regarded as simply arenas for the pursuit of private goods – the criminal justice system, the National Health Service and education. Each of these was shaped in the past by a social vision, often deeply influenced by Christianity. But when vision is eroded, such central social institutions are in danger of becoming harmful, divisive or even demonic.

Social vision, even the most forward-looking, is always a reading or a rereading of the past, and of the narrative canon which presents that past to us – for Christians around the world, the Bible. As such, social vision may lock us into a wistful and maudlin nostalgia, or it may fuel social conflict by excluding the other from our story and making the past a simple conflict between darkness and light. Social visions can be divisive, demeaning and bitter; let there be no doubt about that. They can make us captives of the past, incapable of responding to the challenges of today or the opportunities of tomorrow. But, unless we can possess our past in a proper, realistic and responsible way, we will never be able to cope with the future. And, without an authentic vision, we are hardly likely to be open to the

neighbour and alert to the opportunities and responsibilities which lie to hand.

A Christian vision is inescapably social, precisely
because all the great images of salvation and of the future
in the Christian tradition are models of conviviality,
living together in mutual delight and responsibility – the
Reign of God, the New Jerusalem, the city and so on. It
is a vision of a community of neighbours, remembering
the expansive and rich content that the Bible gives to the
term *neighbour*.

In Britain in the past, crises and conflicts acted as
catalysts for social vision, and religion usually provided
the imagery and the language. Thus Scottish Chartists
in the nineteenth century demanding fundamental
citizenship rights marched to their meetings bearing
Covenanters' banners and singing metrical psalms! It
is my conviction that intellectuals and academics do
not often generate social vision. But when vision
emerges from situations of conflict, suffering and pain,
from the places where vision is renewed, theologians and
academics and clergy may articulate and criticise visions;
indeed, they have a responsibility to do so.

Today in Britain, the church declines numerically and
religious language and symbols seem to many to be tired,
jaded, jejune and esoteric. And yet it was in Edinburgh
that Margaret Thatcher chose to deliver her 'Sermon on
the Mound', and Tony Blair makes frequent reference
to his commitment to Christian Socialism. Are these
things perhaps reminders that religious language has not
in fact lost its currency, and indeed is not as devalued as
is the language of political ideologies? Again and again,
we seem to be driven back to religious language and
find even in Britain what Austin Farrer in a notable book
on Revelation called 'a rebirth of images'.[25] Are the
symbols and the narratives of the Bible still capable of

serving as vehicles for renewed and lively social visions of conviviality and hope? Can we rescue and renew a shared and hospitable Christian social vision, which is open to the future and generates goals and motivation for the twenty-first century? Can Christianity in today's Britain criticise and assess the visions on offer? Is Christianity still capable of pointing to a vision of the future which will draw people together in seeking justice, fellowship, truth and human flourishing?

Ultimately, for Christians, true vision is the vision of God and of fellowship in and with the Triune God. The church is called to be a kind of preliminary manifestation or earnest (*arrabon* = down-payment) of that vision. That does not mean that the church or theology generate or devise the Christian vision. But they have a responsibility to discern it, and explore it, and manifest it, and proclaim it. In the New Testament, the visions were not visions of the glorious future of the church, but of a new heaven and a new earth, the renewal of the whole world, a New Jerusalem in which there will be no church or temple, but God will be all in all. Thus we are constantly reminded that judgment begins with the household of faith, the community that nurtures and commends the Christian vision. For we are stewards, not possessors, of the Christian vision.

Prophecy

He who would do good to another, must do it in minute particulars

General good is the plea of the scoundrel, hypocrite and flatterer.[26]

Prophecy is the application of vision to a particular situation. It is always specific and particular. Prophecy wrestles with particular problems and issues within the horizon of a vision. It demonstrates, as it were, the cash value, the relevance of the vision; it earths the vision in what William Blake called 'minute particulars', it makes it operative in a particular situation. Without prophecy, it is hardly possible to grasp the vision except as an escapist pipe-dream which has no bearing on the world – vacuous general statements rather than specific demands. True prophecy is disturbing because it challenges the dominant values and the conventional wisdom of the age. We need constantly to unpack the bearing of vision on specifics, for the concrete here means the actual points where people are hurting and the issues that press upon their reality. This is precisely what Martin Luther King did in the midst of the civil-rights struggle when he proclaimed: 'I have a dream . . . every valley shall be exalted, and every hill shall be made low . . . we will be free one day.' And more recently in the twentieth century, Archbishop Tutu, Oscar Romero and many others proclaimed their Christian social vision with great courage.

I do not wish to suggest that it is easy or uncontentious to attempt to unpack the bearing of vision on specifics. Far from it. But this is surely a central task of public theology, which cannot be shirked. For, without the hard and difficult endeavour to move from vision to the specifics of prophecy, what claims to be prophecy easily becomes a mere recycling of the favoured slogans of the moment without distinctive Christian – and there-fore gospel – content, or, at the other extreme, theological pronouncements which have no bearing on the specifics of the issue under consideration. Much that claims to be prophecy seems to have little if any theological content, and to be hardly related at all to the Christian vision.

The worship of the church is at least potentially prophetic, both a witness to the vision and a disturbing challenge to the specific injustices and untruthfulness of the context in which it is set. Prophecy is thus an unavoidable ecclesiastical and theological responsibility. A public theology which declines to prophesy is in a state of dereliction of its duty. And a faithful social theology usually starts from specific issues, situations in which people are hurting and being oppressed. It does not impose some 'theory of everything' on the issues, but attends to the insights and challenges which arise from the issue, and then searches to discover if there are theological fragments which may be offered, which may give insight, encouragement and challenge to those wrestling with the issue.

Theological Fragments

Public theology needs to learn how to concern itself with the concrete and the specific, with the particular needs of neighbours, far and near. Commitment to great moral or political systems and ideals can sometimes conflict directly with an ethical attitude to the concrete other, as in Dostoevsky's doctor, who said:

> I love humanity, . . . but I wonder at myself. The more I love humanity in general, the less I love man [sic] in particular. In my dreams . . . I have often come to making enthusiastic schemes for the service of humanity, and perhaps I might actually have faced crucifixion if it had been suddenly necessary; and yet I am incapable of living in the same room with anyone for two days together, as I know by experience . . . In twenty-four hours I begin to hate the best of men . . . But it has always happened that the more I detest men individually the more ardent becomes my love for humanity.[27]

In its concern with the concrete, with action and existence, and with freedom, and in its suspicion of grandiose and impersonal schemes and systems, post-modernity presents opportunities and challenges to the mission of the church. Indeed, the recognition of fragmentation opens a whole range of evangelistic opportunities.

I have suggested the deployment of 'theological fragments' not because I buy into the post-modernist scenario (although I find it quite illuminating, particularly in its view of grand theories as oppressive), but because in a situation where most people are both ignorant and suspicious of Christian doctrine and practice there is really no other way forward than presenting or offering 'fragments' which may be seen as relevant and true, illuminating and helpful for just practice.

A theologian should not, I think, be ashamed of offering initially in public debate in the conditions of post-modernity no more than 'fragments' of insight. Post-modernists (and sociologists of knowledge) are after all right in affirming that systematic, carefully developed theories can sometimes conceal practices which are inhumane and brutalising. Ideologies can serve as the emperor's new clothes, so that the theologian's task, as a little child, is to cry out: 'But the emperor's got no clothes on!': a fragment of truth reveals that to which most people have allowed themselves to be blinded. Truth-telling in a fragmentary way becomes even more important when the scheme to conceal the emperor's nakedness is something that is hurting people and destroying community.[28]

Moral and theological fragments come from specific quarries, or visions if you prefer that terminology. We know that theological fragments by which Christians live and which shape their practice have their home in a community of shared faith, the church, which, if it is true to its calling and its mission, does not wistfully look back to an unrecoverable past, but looks forward with expectation to God's future, and meanwhile offers its fragments as a contribution to the common store and seeks to embody its insights in its life. Only at the end will the fragments, the 'puzzling reflections in a mirror', give way to a face-to-face encounter with the Truth.

When a fragment is recognised as in some sense true, one should expect an interest in its provenance, in its embeddedness in a broader truth. Is a compelling task and opportunity today the bringing together of 'theological fragments' which have been illuminating, instructive or provocative in grappling with issues of practice 'on the ground', reflecting on them, and on their embeddedness in the structure of Christian faith, and enquiring whether this gives clues as to a constructive contribution in the public realm today? This may well be the way towards the renewal and recovery of Christian social vision in the conditions of today.

By 'fragments' I mean a wide range of things – the importance of forgiveness in any decent criminal justice system, confessional statements such as the 1934 Theological Declaration of Barmen which established the German Confessing Church in opposition to Nazism, Frank Field's suggestion that a 'Christian' view of human nature is necessary for a viable welfare system, and many others. Fragments may be irritants (the grit in the oyster that gathers a pearl?), stories/parables, the Socratic questioning of received assumptions, even the 'road metal' for straight paths.

Fragments, of course, come from somewhere; they have been quarried. My purpose in talking this way about real happenings and possibilities is partly evangelical: some people who recognise a Christian fragment as true may trace it back to the quarry from which it comes. But I am also increasingly aware that fragments detached from the quarry are particularly liable to be abused or misunderstood and distorted. Thus the theological task is, I believe, twofold: injecting or offering theological fragments in public debate and, simultaneously, labouring in the quarry or mine – work that may be largely invisible and regarded by most as irrelevant, but which is in fact essential. This, I believe, is precisely how Barth behaved in the 1930s: hard, unrelenting work on the Dogmatics 'as if nothing had happened' (his phrase), and simultaneously bombarding the Nazis and the German Christians with a fusillade of fragments which for many people provided a strong discernment of what was actually happening, and how a Christian should respond. What I am profoundly opposed to is a facile presentation of idealistic commonplaces as if they were theological fragments!

Another parallel analogy which in some ways is a corrective to the fragments and quarry image, and is far more deeply rooted in Christian thought and liturgical practice, is that of the loaf and the crumbs or grains. The separate grains are ground and kneaded and baked into bread, the one loaf which is the sign of the Body of Christ, both the body broken on the Cross and the body of believers who gather and are dispersed in the world to bring forth fruit. For the work of salvation, for the work of God in the world, the body/loaf must be broken into crumbs, only to be gathered together into one at the end of time. At the heart of Christian faith and action is the breaking of the bread for the nourishment of God's people. The crumbs are food for a pilgrim people.

Some fragments are like pieces of glass or gems that catch the light and display its wonderful colours, or generate a vision that many can share – glimpses into another world. It is perhaps better that visions and hopes of utopias should be generated in this way than by one of the huge ideologies that seem now to have collapsed.

People and societies need to be liberated from being confined in the prison of 'the real world', unable to dream the dreams which will shape the practice of tomorrow and become ultimately the practice of the Reign of God.

So back to the quarry, to obtain the fragments that give us road metal, that provoke the oyster to make pearls, that concentrate the light into visions, that generate utopias, that build up jigsaws of meaning, and that nourish the activity of truthfulness, love and justice which is the practice of the Reign of God!

Notes

1. Václav Havel, *Living in Truth*, London: Faber, 1987. The parable of the greengrocer is to be found on pp. 41ff.
2. Karl Barth, *The Knowledge of God and the Service of God according to the Teaching of the Reformation*, London: Hodder & Stoughton, 1938.
3. Ibid., p. 104.
4. Karl Barth, *A Letter to Great Britain from Switzerland*, London: Sheldon, 1941, p. 14.
5. Ibid., p. 15.
6. Ibid., p. 17.
7. See my 'Reformed radical orthodoxy: can it be retrieved?' in *Truthful Action: Explorations in Practical Theology*, Edinburgh: T&T Clark, 2000, pp. 161–84.
8. On the development of the idea of royal supremacy in the early English reformation, see especially Diarmid MacCulloch, *Thomas Cranmer*, New Haven: Yale University Press, 1996, esp. pp. 278, 349, 364, 576f. and 617.
9. D. B. Forrester and D. Skene, eds, *Just Sharing: A Christian Approach to the Distribution of Wealth, Income and Benefits*, London: Epworth, 1988.
10. And discussed more fully in chapter 11 of my *Truthful Action: Explorations in Practical Theology*, Edinburgh: T&T Clark, 2000.
11. James K. Cameron, ed., *The First Book of Discipline*, Edinburgh: Saint Andrew Press, 1972.
12. See *Truthful Action*, pp. 174–8.

13. This section is adapted from chapter 9 of my *Truthful Action: Explorations in Practical Theology*, Edinburgh: T&T Clark, 2000.
14. Matthew 12:38–42 and 16:1–4; Luke 11:16, 29–32; Mark 8:11–12.
15. Karl Barth, *Theological Existence Today*, ET, London: Hodder & Stoughton, 1933, pp. 9–10.
16. Proverbs 31:8–9.
17. This is a process which reminds us of David Hume's famous saying, 'Reason is, and ought to be, the slave of the passions'. But we are suggesting particular kinds of passion that reason should serve.
18. Edited by Duncan B. Forrester and Danus Skene, London: Epworth Press, 1988.
19. See Chris Wood, *The End of Punishment: Christian Perspectives on the Crisis in Criminal Justice*, Edinburgh: CTPI, 1991; *Law and Order – Prospects for the Future*, CTPI Occasional Paper No. 10, 1986; *Justice, Guilt and Forgiveness in the Penal System*, Occasional Paper No. 18, 1990; *Penal Policy: The Way Forward*, Occasional Paper No. 27, 1991.
20. Order of Excommunication and of Public Repentance, in John Cumming, ed., *The Liturgy of the Church of Scotland, or John Knox's Book of Common Order*, London: J. Leslie, 1840, pp. 140–1, 145, 148.
21. Edinburgh: CTPI Occasional Paper No. 12, 1987.
22. Edited by Andrew Morton, Edinburgh: CTPI Occasional Paper No. 43, 1998.
23. The sections on vision and prophecy are adapted from chapter 10 of my book, *Truthful Action*.
24. Habakkuk 2:2–3.
25. Austin Farrer, *A Rebirth of Images: The Making of St John's Apocalypse*, London: Dacre Press, 1949; Gloucester, MA: Peter Smith, 1970.
26. William Blake, *Jerusalem*, chapter 3.
27. F. Dostoevsky, *The Brothers Karamazov*, London: Heinemann, 1912, pp. 52–3.
28. Notice that Z. Bauman characterises 'the post-modern perspective' as 'above all the tearing off of the mask of illusions; the recognition of certain pretences as false and certain objectives as neither attainable or, for that matter, desirable' (*Post-Modern Ethics*, p. 3).

Part III

Doing Social Theology: Listening to Different Voices

The different voices can be seen as awkward and threatening by the majority, or as of utmost importance. Methodologically, they warn against foreclosing debate and embracing easy solutions. Such warnings are vital within the context of church and university, the usual settings for theological work.

The principles of doing social theology within 'local communities' throw up major challenges. Both practically and in ideological terms, new ways of coming together and strengthening relationships demand considerable investments of time and energy. The church has a learning task here, to establish its true role and to break free of various inherited handicaps. The building of trust and the achievement of social transformation, be it in small advances or great leaps, requires patience and persistence. But the question is well raised of where the focus of action should lie. Church in its historical reality, with all the attendant weaknesses, and also tendencies which run against the nurturing of close and sufficiently small community commitments, form a very critical part of the picture.

As well as people of the church needing to think through and perhaps very radically reassess their calling within local communities, the task of the university theologian is also bound to take note of the importance of 'difference'. In the next two chapters here, there are powerful reflections on the mixture of passions and identities and the need to break out of any assumed 'sameness', because there are issues which 'demand our attention and struggle' (Althaus-Reid). The theologians may have something to give, but they also have a great deal to learn. They have to enter into dialogue with those who speak differently or who perhaps speak very little; and there is the whole arena of music and the creative arts. An ecumenism of spirit is the corollary of the ecumenism, in the widest sense of the term, which lies at the heart of the churches' calling.

It matters to be aware of how fear for survival may blunt the cutting edge of daring to be different and to listen to different voices. An oral contribution closely connected with all of this told how, in the light of disturbing revelations of hurt within the church – in this case uncensured violence against women – the presenter was branded as 'an embittered feminist with an axe to grind'. Though intended presumably as an insult, it named very well something absolutely vital – an anti-social, protest dimension in the doing of social theology.

One other significant arena for listening is that of the arts. Visually, aurally and in words, the input of the arts embraces, as Willy Slavin puts it, 'dimensions . . . open to a wider epiphany'. The churches have had a very mixed impact historically on the working of creative spirits, a point true enough in our own time when it is less than common for artists to pursue explicitly Christian themes. No doubt there may be as many contrasting threads as common threads to unravel, but the theological task would be greatly impoverished were these 'voices' not to be heeded. The inclusion of a few verbal contributions from outwith the conventional theological fold gives a taster of what is there to be explored.

It was the women who with their will still intact, with thanks not to their religion but to a matriarchal tradition, who tried longest to withstand the clearances after their men had been destroyed by their chiefs.

Hamish Henderson, from *Alias MacAlias*

5

Veníamos de Otras Tierras

A Reflection on Diasporas, Liberation Theology and Scotland

Marcella Althaus-Reid

> In the year of the death of President Allende
> And the war in the Middle East . . .
> I felt the presence of the Lord,
> Commander in Chief of the Cosmic Armies
> And without any doubt, the Lord of History.
> The tanks, convoys and warplanes
> Looked to me as if they were extraterrestrial beings
> . . .
> I was scared and said:
> Oh, help! I'm lost!
> Look, I am a man who doesn't have weapons,
> Not even a grenade,
> And I live in a poor country, exploited
> And without food resources . . .
>
> Ernesto Cardenal, *Psalm 130*

Veníamos de otras tierras. We came from other lands. We came from the South. We were Others coming from the lands of the Others. Some of us were women. Some women had fled the Pinochet regime or the Argentinian Junta or whatever menacing force was there, threatening their lives. Fate put us together in Scotland. We spoke Spanish, mixing our different pronunciations, using different words for the same things and pondering

our different rhythms and ways to say things. We came
from different cultures and nationalist struggles; also
with full complex lives formed in the arenas of political
confrontation. Some of us came with a Christian faith
nurtured in militant churches back home and informed
by liberation theology.

Talking with some friends one winter afternoon in a
flat in Dundee, I spontaneously remembered some lines
of Jeremiah which I knew then by heart:

> Yes. A groan of pain comes from Sion: Oh, to think that
> we are so ruined and ashamed! To have had to abandon
> our nation (*la patria*), and to see our homes destroyed!
> You, women, listen to this word of YHWH, listen to the
> word from God's mouth. Teach your daughters this mourn-
> ing song, and teach each other this lamentation: Death has
> come through our windows and entered into our houses;
> death has taken the life of the child in the street, and the
> young people in the public parks. There are bodies lying in
> the country . . . there is nobody to bury them.[1]

We were used to reading the Bible as if the Scriptures
were letters from our own mothers: a retelling of what
we had been through, and words of comfort and assur-
ance that, in the end, God's justice will prevail. The Bible
was so factual; after all, death had come in some cases
literally through our windows, as the paramilitaries were
known for seldom ringing doorbells. Some of the women
who were gathered that afternoon in Dundee were,
after all, part of that youth who managed to escape from
the burning of Bibles in the public parks to the carnage
of the football stadiums of Latin America. Reading
Jeremiah among ourselves was easy because sometimes
it was as if the Bible was quoting and interpreting us,
and not the other way round. This happened many
years ago, when we were younger and our wounds
fresher. It was the time when some of us felt that the

only belongings we had were a handful of Psalms, which we quoted stubbornly, obsessively, provoking the curiosity of several church ministers in Fife. This was a long time ago – yet any reflection about theology and the public issues concerning liberation in Scotland needs for me to start precisely there, at that point of the Diaspora not of an imported Latin American theology, but of the people of the militant churches of the South.

We could start by asking ourselves simple questions. For instance, who reads the Bible today as if it was her own mother's letters? Who mourns what today? Are we still Christians in Exodus? Have we forgotten that nothing is settled yet in this building process of the Kingdom, although the global ethics of Capitalism tells us that there are no alternatives to the God of the Market? I may not be able to reply to all of these questions in this chapter, but it will be important to set a theological framework from which, eventually, we may wish to respond to them.

Theology and Ideology: Combinations

There are two things which are still very important in considering a reflection of theology and public issues. One is theology, and the other is ideology, and neither of these, separately or combined, can be considered to be stable terms. Someone could argue that culture is an important third element in the debate; but, from a materialist perspective, let us assume culture is part of a discourse of ideology.

The point is one of how these elements combine among themselves. As I have said before, we may have come from other lands (and other ideologies), but not as a homogeneous group. Among ourselves, as Latin Americans for instance, the combinations of theology and ideology were different. Our cultures were different too, even if belonging to the same countries. There were several quite unique combinations in each person, made up of beliefs in religious and economic myths, plus issues of class and sexual identities and learned affective traditions. We came to Scotland to live in council estates and deprived areas, yet the poor in Scotland had incorporated different combinations of theology and ideology in their lives. We did not always understand each other. Perhaps what happened then was that, somehow, in the midst of these encounters among strangers, liberation theology went into a Diaspora in our lives; Christian people were encountering the different, and learning lessons about change.

I remember, for instance, that one (middle-class) Pentecostal church in Dundee suddenly found the disturbing presence in their midst of a poor Pentecostal family from Latin America, who had suffered political persecution due to working in a trade union. Pentecostalism and trade-union struggles represented a hybrid identity among those Scottish Christian people. Personally, I learnt two words: one was 'evangelical' and the other was 'liberal'. You were supposed to be on this side or the other, but it was difficult. I was another kind of hybrid, labelled a 'liberal Christian' who never started a day without reading the Bible. Strange combinations (or the combinations of strangers) in theology and ideology always tend to produce unexpected Christian reflections and renewals, even if confusing at times.

In theology, as in people's lives, there are also times of Diaspora and change in the multiple combinations or co-ordinates of the theological and ideological discourses. Sometimes we fail by ignoring the complexity that our analysis requires. In Latin American theology, for instance, that criticism from Althusser concerning using only a 'touch of class' to do philosophy (or theology, we may add) has, unfortunately, been a reality.[2] Stressing class analysis (as the one and privileged ideological system to ground our theology), Liberationists had forgotten what else may be due to the reflection of a theology using serious doubt as a hermeneutical circle, in the pursuit of God in justice and solidarity. José Comblin, in one of his most recent books *Call to Freedom*, has produced a criticism of this blindness in liberation theology towards the complexity of ideological systems. For instance, liberation theology ignored the deep issues of sexual ideology which permeate Latin American societies, creating cultural and political covenants of exploitation and injustice in the lives of many of our people. Meanwhile, to use another example, we can say that feminist theology in the North Atlantic scene seldom used class analysis in its reflection on God and gender issues. Race has been and still is much ignored as an active component in theological reflections. Although issues of race have been powerfully put at the forefront of theology since the 1970s, such theological work still remains marginal and fragmentary because the main corpus of systematic theology has never taken it seriously. That means that we can teach or refer to black or womanist theology, but as theologies *apart* from the main corpus of teaching christology or eschatology. There has not been a consistent effort to reflect theologically using the full circle of ideological suspicion. By keeping class, gender, sexuality and race marginal (as particular developments at the borders of the main corpus of theology), we have made them ineffective. We have exiled them.

However, the problem becomes evident when we want to do a theology of public issues. That may be problematic because, in the public issues we want to reflect on, we will find that permanently, and without stability, different ideological trends combine together. For instance, in the debate on Clause 28 in Scotland, the political discussion was informed by a heterosexual ideology combined with a liberal family standpoint. 'The family' (which is always the Trojan horse of any theological/political debate) was not seen as what it is, a particular form of social organisation. It was not considered that the family is a kinship form which does not necessarily need to be organised around biological and reproductive issues, as Juliette Mitchell has demonstrated in her studies on gender and families.[3] Valuable kinship relations can also develop outside relations of profit, as shown by the example of Jesus Christ, who chose not to reproduce himself. Paraphrasing Elizabeth Stuart, we can say that families do not need to follow the work ethic of our present capitalist system.[4] Contrary to the dictum of global capitalism, no non-profit relationship should ever need to be excluded from society.

The Indifferent Theologian

It is interesting to consider that, as Marx said, ideologies are methods, not final products.[5] In the brief example of the debate on Clause 28, there is a whole exegesis of the heterosexual family against the friendships of those outside these definitions which also remind us of processes of global exclusion. As it is with definitions of family, deciding who is there and who is not, so it is with society. As materialist theologians know, there are no innocent discourses in the politics of interpreting the Bible or our societies; but, if we took this point even further, we might see how, more than ever, doing theology and public issues requires choosing our understanding of ideologies in all their complexity. The Marxist reflection on ideology as a method leads us to consider Diaspora, exodus and points of continuing departing while joining 'other caravans' in our doing theology today, in the circumstances of the life of our nations. What we need is to recognise the level of exchange between theologies and ideologies among us, in two ways. First, we need to recognise the disturbing presence of people and concepts in Diaspora which may appear in our midst, and allow them to participate in our dialogue on equal terms. Second, we need to recognise that ideology, as a method, is institutionally located. What we need is a new liberation of theology (as in the cry of the late Juán Luis Segundo during the 1970s) – but the problem is that theology cannot be liberated if it does not challenge the institutionalised ideology which constrains its path. Is being a theologian the same as being an administrator (or any other worthy yet different *profession*)? Can a theologian fulfil her vocation under the current organisational and financial procedures of our university policies? How do we assess, evaluate and administer prophecy? Can theology ever partake of this assumed 'sameness'?

It is obvious that the goals and objectives of any *sameness* project move towards the production of precisely 'the same' (not the prophetic). Sameness will make of us *indifferent* theologians, or theologians making difference when confronting public issues which demand our attention and struggle. What rebelliousness, what different values then can be nurtured and allowed to grow there? Do the church and the academic institutions of divinity manufacture desires for sameness that later condemn us as lacking in prophecy and Christian vision? With what methodological (ideological) trap are theology and public issues confronted here?

The point is that doing theology and public issues cannot be related to an ethos of *sameness* but, on the contrary, to the careful articulation of the different and the silenced in the official discourses of mass media and church alike. This also includes a different theological vision to be manifested in the way that we are going to fulfil our duty to train a new generation of Scottish theologians for the near future. I started this brief reflection by recounting the days of life in Scotland, as a land of exile for some Christian people in whose lives theology and political struggles may have been part of a common process. For some of them, church and theology was then made by militancy and gestures of defiance against hegemonic economic systems. Those economic systems left many theologians in Latin America without jobs and promotion, as well as friends and peace in their lives. I like to think about them with love and gratitude. I am proud to have met what in Scotland may have been called 'extravagant theologians' who, by many small gestures of defiance, rebelliousness and non-conformism, taught us to refuse to support, encourage or obey any project of *sameness* imposed upon us. Although times have changed, politically and otherwise, it may be good for us to remember that valuable praxis of our elders, and to consider if the moment has not come for us to reflect on a whole new liturgical act of gestures of defiance against the sameness trend of many educational institutions. We are at the moment when globalisation processes threaten us with the sins of conformity, without alternatives and demanding that administrative efficiency be shown in our theology as in our theological institutions. More than ever, we must persist in talking theology and public issues as a movement, not a final product. No metaphysics of accountancy can ever evaluate what we consider our call to build with God his Kingdom of

Justice. A theology of public issues must be affirmed as a way to discern in the light of God the complex web of ideology and theology in public discourse and to provide us with alternatives. This, however, can only be done if we dare to think theology first of all, from all the angles of marginality in our societies, and second by reflecting in the locus of ideology and theology today.

Only in this way might we be able to discern who is reading what in the Bible today; or who is mourning what, while welcoming all the readings of all the mourners of our nations: the cry of the poor, or women, or men without hope, or people marginalised by sexuality or race. This, in itself, may prove to be the biggest act of resistance to the current process of globalisation of capitalism which would like to make us believe that the promise of the Kingdom, after all, fell with some forms of socialism, and is an issue for the history books. And this is precisely what we need, honouring God: a theology of public issues denying that the ultimate Christian alternative, which is the project of the Kingdom, has failed.

Notes

1. This is a literal translation of Jeremiah 10:18–21 from the Spanish. See *La Biblia Latinoamericana*, Madrid: Paulinas, 1972.
2. I have further developed this point on Althusser in my book *Indecent Theology: Theological Perversions in Sex, Gender and Politics*, London: Routledge, 2000, p. 25.
3. See Juliette Mitchell, *Psychoanalysis and Feminism*, New York: Vintage Press, 1974, pp. 379–80.
4. From a remark made by Professor Stuart during the series of the Cunningham Lectures, New College, February 2001.
5. For a further development of this point, see my article '*¿Bien Sonados?* The future of mystical connections in liberation theology', in *Political Theology* (3), November 2000.

Scrabster, or Skarabolstadr in old Norse,
means (as I learned)
the standing at the edge.

There in that harbour on the north
coast of Scotland, facing
the awful power of the Pentland Firth
and the North Atlantic,
you inhale a certain metaphysic –
an exhilarating liberation
(if the gale doesn't blow you over)
from the centripetal force
of our monstrous civilisation.

It's not the call of the unknown
that made bold sailors quit
the safety of the old continent in frail
caravels five centuries ago.
It's not the curious economy of surface –
the globe and our flat knowledge of it –
that confronts the mystic on the shores of
California, gazing westwards towards the east.
The ocean here conveys a more immediate,
elementary intelligence.

Alastair Hulbert, 'Standing at the Edge',
in *The Gift Half Understood: essays on a European journey*

6

Doing Social Theology with the Excluded

Malcolm Cuthbertson

'Doing social theology' is the committed activity in, reflection on, and celebration of, along with others, especially the excluded, the positive transformation of all levels of social relationships, the means and end goal of which is to create and sustain community throughout humanity, and between humanity and creation, as prefigured in the Christian understanding of Trinity and in the activity and teaching of Jesus Christ.

Doing social theology requires an active commitment to be involved in the social processes of one or more levels of social relationships, including our relationship with the physical environment. There clearly has to be a recognition that social theology is about relationships between individuals and groups of individuals, whether at the level of neighbourhood, community, local authority district, nation, society or indeed world. A specific commitment to a group of people and the process of transformation is important. A commitment to some very specific relationships earths the activity and theology in the real world with real people. A commitment alongside others already helps to create and sustain community which acts both as a sign for future achievements that may be sought and also as a support through activity that may be long-term and sacrificial of time and energy. The motivation and vision for the drive towards community arises out of the Christian understanding of God as Trinity. The God who is worshipped is already a community who inspires and challenges humankind to reflect the image of the triune God. The strategy is one of incarnation. Jesus commits himself to a particular people in a particular place at a particular time. He seeks from within that context to exemplify in word and action the agenda of God, building communion and community and challenging those individuals and institutions that would seek to exclude or marginalise, to change their ways. Out of the particularity of the incarnation come the universals of gospel imperatives which we are asked to implement in our own contexts.

The doing of social theology is itself a social activity to be done with others. It is clearly understood that there is an intimate connection between the personal and the social, such that the personal will inevitably impact the social and the social will also impact at a personal level. Nevertheless, social theology is about participating with others in the transformation of society, and the physical environment, which is itself part of personal and social redemptive activity. One's participation with another or others enhances and fulfils our need and desire for social relationships. In this, one is already experiencing community which is the goal of social theology. The establishing and sustaining of such relationships also, as mentioned above, become active signs of the redemptive process for others. Outsiders can see from one's committed relationships the possibilities and potential for themselves. The movement out of isolation and marginalisation is prefigured for others in one's own committed relationships. More practically, the awareness of the complexity of social relationships at all levels, and the manifold needs of individuals, groups and nations to relate better and to care better for the world, necessitates a communal and corporate approach to the transformation process. The level of energy, emotion and time, and the differing skills, abilities and experience required for social transformation cannot be held in one person, community or nation. The lone-ranger approach to social transformation is barren and futile. This partnership with others already begins to highlight the need for transformation and redemption. The appreciation that those others one needs to relate to are different from oneself already throws up the potential, not only for community, but also for conflict.

Doing social theology is about creating, enhancing and celebrating the process by which people, or peoples, join with other people or peoples to create relationships of mutual acceptance and belonging, and also joint creative purposes for future communal activity. Due to the pull of egocentricity or xenophobia apparent in the history of humankind, social relationships have not always been entered into or continued on the basis of friendship and mutual acceptance and respect. Nor have they always accomplished joint actions towards the enhancement of communal relationships internally among their own members or externally with outsiders. (If they had, of course, there would have been little need for God's actions of redemption in either the Old or New Testaments.) Power differentials across a range of issues, for example economic, political, sexual and intellectual, have opened up, with the ultimate power being the power to decide who is in and who is not, that is, who receives the benefit of membership of, and contribution to, a particular community, and who does not. Clearly, such powers may be used beneficially, for example scape-goating in the Old Testament (cf. Isaiah 53) or excommunication, both of which sought positively to enhance the community by renouncing the anti-social behaviour of the community or of elements within the community. While such activity as the latter may be seen as punishment, more likely was the understanding that anti-social behaviour may be contagious, but also more crucially, the hope that a period outwith the community, such as imprisonment, may lead to repentance and full restoration back into the community at some point in the future. More marked, however, is the way in which the power differentials have created across the social spectrum a series of individuals, groups and nations who feel marginalised, isolated and excluded. Barriers between rich and poor, black and white, Catholic and Protestant, Christian and Muslim, male and female, heterosexual and homosexual, and many more, are all too apparent in our communities and across the world. The need for the Gospel of reconciliation is perfectly clear.

Doing social theology leads to an active commitment to and with those who are excluded. The practical reason for this is the issue of perspective. It is extremely difficult, and some would argue impossible, for the person who is part of the group which sets the social norms, put in place largely for the contentment of those who help to establish normative behaviour, to understand and appreciate those who are excluded by those same social norms. There is still a significant problem when those who are the powerful initiate change even from the best of motives. Thus, for the process of redemption and reconciliation, the primary perspective that has to be understood is that of the individual or group that is excluded. Those who do social theology need to find these people, if they are not already members with them, and help the process of social analysis and theological reflection as to their exclusion, and act with them, and if necessary, against the powerful norm-setters, to create or recreate full membership and participation of those excluded, alongside those who had previously set the norms. There can be no acceptance of the situation whereby the power is simply transferred from one party to another since there has been no movement towards community, but simply the replacement of excluder by the excluded, who then becomes the excluder. The specifics of this process will be unique to each situation, and the members will determine how it is to be done in the context. In simple issues, a highlighting of the exclusion may well be enough to change the situation for the better, or at other times it may take years of violence before reconciliation prevails, while in between, in some kind of continuum, education and political action may also be part of the process.

Doing social theology is a major problem for Western Christendom, and indeed may be impossible. The so-called 'first world' of the West is quite clearly the dominant force in setting the norms for the rest of the world. The Western church has become so closely allied to this dominant perspective that its ability to see from the perspective of the marginalised or excluded is entirely questionable. Indeed, some of those who are clearly experiencing exclusion may well be doing so as a result of the church's own behaviour. In the light of this, the doing of social theology becomes extremely difficult and is as much a critique of the church as it is of any other group, community or nation. There have thankfully been some people outwith the church who have played a significant role in bringing about community, while those who have tried to do so from within the church have often been vilified or practically excommunicated from their positions of leadership or even membership.

The challenge for those who seek to do social theology is also to understand and analyse within the Christian community the social processes that have led to exclusion, and work to restore a measure of integrity and community to the church.

Doing Social Theology in a Local Community

Difficulties immediately arise when one tries to place the principles set out above in the context of the local community – whatever that is. Clearly, the term 'local' suggests a geographical locality that is smaller than national. This could be really anything from a neighbourhood as small as a few houses to a burgh or local-authority district. However, while one's residential address may determine the geographical locality with which one can be identified, it is nowhere near identifying the sense or feeling of community to which one is attached. For example, a resident of Easterhouse in Glasgow may in fact work in another locality, have leisure activity in another community, have family commitments in another community, and still yet seek to define himself by where he was born, his religious affiliation, and of course the football team for which he has a season ticket! How is community to be defined for such a person? Even in more mixed communities such as suburban parishes, while church attendance from within the parish may be strong, there may still be a large commitment to travelling to attend church; and, with increased mobility in terms of car ownership and even public transport, the need to be local for work or leisure is no longer strong.

While at a cultural level some schools, churches and families, particularly where grandparents are close, may educate their children about the local community in terms of its customs, history and physical environment, the increasing centralisation of the school curriculum and the almost overwhelming influence of the media and their use by marketing professionals make it more likely that children may know more about New York than their own village or town, or about American basketball players than their local football team.

Once again, the critical issue becomes one of attachment or commitment. Most people will identify as their community that to which they give the greatest attachment in terms of time, energy, emotion and other resources. That may be a local neighbourhood or community, or indeed the nation. It may also be an issue-based or value-based community such as the church, the Labour Party or the local athletics club. For those who wish to do social theology in a local community, the desire to bring about social change requires a commitment to the community that may be changed. The importance, and even preference, for doing social theology at this local level cannot be overestimated. Involvement at national level with national concerns, while needed, can be an escape from real involvement with real people in real issues at the micro level. This involvement at the grassroots also becomes the building blocks for national or international campaigns and programmes. Unless coming in as a consultant in the process, such change as anticipated above will rarely be achieved without some kind of attachment over a period of time.

For the church, and particularly local churches whether at parish or regional level which claim local allegiance, the need for a specific commitment to the local community needs to be made clear. In the majority of congregations, presbyteries and so on, the contents of their worship and business meetings are largely without context and could be moved to anywhere in Scotland if not the Western world. To be context-specific is not a weakness of the church but rather a strength. Of course, the main commitment of members of the Christian church need not be to specific locality-based communities. They may belong to other communities of interest or value-based communities such as workplaces or social clubs, and the institutional church may also be represented by industrial, prison, hospital or school-based chaplaincies. However, whether one's commitment lies in the locality-based community or elsewhere, the role for those who seek to do social theology is the same. This is the search to build community and social relationships, especially across social barriers and from the perspective of the excluded and marginalised. The real danger, to which the present church is inclined, is that the communities to which we are committed are not in fact part of the pressure for change, but rather are there to promote the stability and social cohesion of its membership – and most wish and work for it to remain that way. The church and professional chaplaincies may collude in this process by sanctifying the status quo. This has become even more evident where institutions and not the church specifically hire the chaplain.

There is, in the midst of all this activity and analysis, also the need to sustain the community that is there, and to seek to strengthen relationships. Not all those doing social theology need to be front-line missionaries seeking to remove the barriers of bigotry or race or poverty; some may be back-room workers who hold together and support the community already there. The need for refuge and healing for those who are in pain, and the need of those who more generally need to withdraw from time to time, also have to be taken into account. This sustaining work refreshes activists for the front-line again and should therefore be seen as two sides of the one coin and not as opposing functions within the doing of social theology, although the main thrust will always be towards social transformation.

In the doing of social theology, one should not forget the importance of what has become known as the 'gift economy', those people who devote their time and energy to the community for little or no financial reward. It would appear that the people who are willing to do this may be decreasing due to the rise in the importance of making wealth to enhance life-style, or the rise in home-based entertainments which appear safer and more enjoyable than community service. Hence we see a run-down of many organisations and groups who previously depended on such gifts of time and labour. Social theologians will be part of the example and encouragement of this 'gift economy', as it reflects profoundly the example of Jesus Christ.

While the visionary tasks of promoting communion, community and the personal development required for the purposes of serving the community may be easily understood and accepted, the practical outworking of this agenda will be far from easy. Indeed, from time to time it may well take on the appearance of total failure and chaos. The journey to the promised land as prefigured in the Exodus will be just as trying and will involve the shared experience of highs and lows, and the constant knowledge of the unfinished nature of the work will be inherent in every task.

However, one important building block is the need to celebrate wherever the work is. The church and elements of the non-church community ought to be able to celebrate regularly both the victories achieved, however small, and the diversity already inherent in the community, and to lament failure and loss when it occurs. The church appears to have lost the celebratory function within the local community within its worship context, and should seek to regain it for the benefit of all.

Finally, the choice of doing theology within a local community setting should not forget the importance of the physical environment in which the people are set. Clearly, the materials of earth both in what the earth has naturally in the way of minerals, and of what the earth is able to produce, and even the very issue of land and what it may be used for, have divided peoples for centuries, and no less today. However, there is also the importance of the environment in which we live and work and the importance of beauty and creativity in the natural world to enhance and sustain community, not forgetting the deeper sense of communion with nature available to human beings. Those who seek to do social theology would be shutting out a major factor in social relations were they to concentrate solely on people and not take into account the physical environment in which community is set.

For all the efforts of technology to resist
the limits and authority of nature,
the sea yet marks an end to the land,
to continuity, to the place of our
endeavours – at the end of the day, to culture.
It reminds the willing imagination of that
necessary humility, without which
human constructs are vain.

Nature and time, as they are in
Scrabster, won't be coopted.
They're not partisans of Holyrood,
or Westminister or Brussels.
The sea and the sky and the sound
of sheer silence are an intimation at the edge
of Europe that there's a term to the arrogance
and menace of the Western world.

The wind blows steadily over
Scrabster's cliffs – contradicting the din
of the ten lanes of traffic on the boulevard
where I live. The wind
blows where it wills, and high above
there are the gannets, soaring, watchful,
diving with a desperate hope
against air and sea, worrying a sombre sky
with their stark white purity.

Alastair Hulbert, 'Standing at the Edge',
in *The Gift Half Understood: essays on a European journey*

7

Face-to-face Community

Andrew R. Morton

For me, when talking about community-based theology, 'community' refers particularly to a relatively small group of people, who either live in the same locality or share some other form of common experience or interest; it is a local or at any rate 'micro' community, in contrast to the much larger national, regional or global communities.

Three Comments

Three comments may be apposite. First, such small-scale community is at least *as important* as the larger-scale communities of nation, region and world, and needs to be part of the mix of many levels of community. Second, it is arguably *the most important* form. Third, it is *under threat*.

(1) Culture is shaped by community; identity in turn is shaped by culture; theology in turn is shaped by all three – community, culture and identity – as well as by the Gospel which interacts with them. We tend to recognise that this is so at the macro level such as the nation or region – and so, when we talk about the relationship between gospel and culture, we are thinking of that level, meaning for example 'Western' culture. But it is just as

true of the connections between community, culture, identity and theology at the level of Easterhouse (or Kilsyth, or Edinburgh New Town). So Easterhouse community, culture, identity and theology need to be part of the mix alongside both those of other small-scale communities and those of the larger-scale communities of Scotland, Europe and the world. All communities, small and large, should be thought of as on the level with each other, that is, of equal importance, and should not be arranged vertically or hierarchically as though the smaller were subordinate to the larger. They also need to interact with one another, always in conversation and sometimes in negotiation or even controversy. In such interaction, the small-scale communities should be given as much respect and at least as much attention as the larger ones. So larger-scale communities should not be privileged over smaller-scale ones.

(2) One could go further, for it is arguable that, far from large-scale communities being privileged, small-scale communities should be. The now well-known principle of subsidiarity, which applies to decision-making, states that decisions should be taken as close as possible to the people whom they affect; this gives a bias towards the small-scale group. It is true that it is also part of the notion of subsidiarity that decisions should be taken at the appropriate level, and this does *not* imply a bias towards the small scale; for example, the appropriate level of decision-making on greenhouse gas emissions will be large scale. However, without romanticising what is small as necessarily beautiful, there is something special about a relatively small group, namely its high degree of face-to-faceness. This interpersonal or person-to-person character gives it a particularly rich quality which is rare in a relatively large group. This richness of community in turn enriches the culture, identity and theology which it produces.

So, whether small-scale community is as important as larger-scale community or more important, it is vital. It is essential to human well-being.

(3) Small-scale, face-to-face community, however, is endangered. At best it is neglected or even forgotten; at worst it is undermined or even destroyed. Three processes have been at work – nationalisation, globalisation and individualisation.

Three Trends

Nationalisation

Though the concept of nation goes back several centuries, the nation has become increasingly important in the last 100 years. In that time, the scope of government has expanded greatly, and that growth has been largely at national level. As a result, the sense of national identity has grown. Media of communication have also expanded vastly, and that growth has been largely at national level, with national newspapers and broadcasting. This has further enlarged the sense of national identity. A by-product of 'nationalisation' in this sense has been the eclipse of things local. Whereas in earlier centuries public welfare was a local function (one was 'on the parish') and the first expansion of public utilities in the nineteenth century was municipal, in the twentieth century the utilities were nationalised, income support was moved from the parish to 'national assistance' and then to a national 'Department of Social Security', and a variety of localised health services became an NHS. At the same time, the local newspaper, which was once the main source of information apart from word of mouth, has been overtaken by the national tabloids, broadsheets and broadcasters.

Whatever the pros and cons of this growth of the national dimension of government, communication and identity, one consequence has been to reduce attention to local activity, initiative, decision-making, identity and awareness.

This has been paralleled in church life, at least in the Church of Scotland. Its national identity is far from new, going back to the Reformation and before, and although it is organised at a variety of levels – local, intermediate and national – it has always given precedence to the national, with its General Assembly superior to its other 'courts'. What is new in the last 100 years is the church's imitation of the kind of corporate body or corporation of which the modern national state and modern large enterprise are models. The marks of such a corporation include a bureaucratic structure, a professional staff and a high degree of centralisation. By adopting this form, the church has combined the centralising tendencies of nation and of corporation to the detriment of local initiative, decision-making and vitality.

Globalisation

If this process of nationalisation began around the beginning of the twentieth century, another process, globalisation, is a feature of its end. The word is overused and imprecise, but there would be little dispute that much economic activity has become organised on a very large scale, which takes it far beyond the national level, to say nothing of the local, and moves it at least closer to the global. In addition, there is increasing commodification in the sense that more and more of what we do and what we have is bought and sold. So it is not only that markets are increasingly global but also that more and more of what affects our lives is marketed and therefore part of those globally veering markets. All of this shifts the focus of attention and energy even further away from local and other small-scale communities.

These two trends away from the local – to the national and to the global – combine to reduce local and other small-scale communities politically, economically and culturally, as well as ecclesially. So face-to-face community is being squeezed from 'above'.

Individualisation

However, as great a threat comes to it from 'below'. It may seem paradoxical to say that globalisation is accompanied by individualisation; but it appears to be so. The modern market economy and the philosophical anthropology that supports it are essentially individualist. Their building blocks are individuals, who relate to one another as units, which are separate from one another, uniform with one another and in competition with one another. Globalisation of markets does not change this basic pattern or transform individuals into something that is more than individual; it simply enlarges the field and puts an increasing number of individual units into the same atomistic, homogenising and competitive interplay. The more this marketisation advances, both extensively through the enlargement of its geographical scope and intensively through the commodification of more and more activities, the more it acts as a solvent of community. This was powerfully illustrated in the United Kingdom in the 1980s, when the government of the time vigorously applied this philosophy and systematically undermined communities and institutions which could be described as 'intermediate', that is, between the nation-state and individuals. It is also significant that the advertising of marketable goods and services, which are all now called 'products', is addressed not to communities but to individuals or, at most, to nuclear-family-based households.

So, if small-scale, face-to-face communities are left in the dark of neglect because the spotlight has moved 'up' to the national and the global, they are no less obscured by the spotlight moving 'down' to the individual and the shrinking household.

Now is the time for all – and not least the church – to come to the aid of the face-to-face community.

Nae void can fright me hauf as much
as bein' mysel, whate'er I am
or, worse, bein' onybody else.

Hugh MacDiarmid,
from *A Drunk Man Looks at the Thistle*

8

Social Theology and the Arts

George Newlands

This and the following chapter are concerned with interactions of faith and culture in a number of specific instances. This chapter deals in fragments, and does not intend to demonstrate a grand pattern of fractal similarity beneath the fragments. Most of the fragments are multifaceted, and will be seen differently when examined from different angles. If this study has an ultimate coherence, as it is intended to have, it will be solely the coherence of the shape of the Christian gospel, and this is experienced in worship and service through the centuries. In many of the instances, it will be the darker facets of the fragments which will point to the light.

When we look at the relation between Christianity and the arts, and especially literature, we see an interesting ambiguity in the role of such central images as incarnation, for example in inspiring great poetry and at the same time perhaps in reinforcing authoritarianism in the work of Eliot. Religion and power often go hand in hand, for better and sometimes for worse. Questions of ethics and of truth in corporate and individual life are constantly thrown up by these interdisciplinary explorations, and they require answers, however provisional they may inevitably be.

There are endless different sorts of connections between Christianity, theology and the humanities. Poets and novelists may often be influenced by religious practice and by doctrine, without ever reading formal theology. There are some who did read theology and were consciously influenced by it – Eliot again by Niebuhr and Barth, Auden by Niebuhr and Kierkegaard.

We must note that very different sorts of interactions occur in different cultures. 'Intercultural theology' very often suggests to us inter-religious comparisons across the major world religions and in different continents. But there are also numerous overlapping sub-cultures in European and American societies, and in predominantly Christian contexts. And there is continuous change. It is often said rightly that the Bible has an enormous influence on literature and the humanities. It may be, however, that this influence will be nothing like as great in the next century as it was in the past. It is true that the 'secular Christianity' which many expected in the 1960s to appear did not happen, and the last decades of the twentieth century brought a renewed interest in religion and spirituality in many parts of the world. Yet in Europe at least, church attendance continues to plummet. This distancing from the churches is bound to have an effect on the role of the Bible in society. The novels of the 1980s and 1990s in Europe and even in the United States rarely make Christian or biblical themes central.

Religion and Culture

Religion is embedded in and is part of a complex and fragmented culture. It may be much more than this, a human response to a divine initiative. It is affected by the impact of contemporary cultural trends, at this time globalisation on the one hand and fragmentation on the other. The development of modern mass media assists globalisation. 'Cultural studies' in many university courses has in recent years involved the analysis of 'popular' culture, sometimes in conscious contrast to the 'elite' culture of the European academic tradition. Religion has its place in this revolution, alternately pursued and marginalised by television, and now by the internet. There is not, and perhaps never has been, a single stream of universal culture even in Europe. Knowledge of the older academic tradition cannot be taken for granted in society, though here too there is the phenomenon of particularisation, in which traditional academic guilds are sometimes able to carry on in comparatively insulated circumstances.

Christianity has had much influence on human civilisation, and Christians have been involved in numerous professions. Theologians have of course made available a distinctive contribution.

It is not hard to discover a relationship between personal belief and professional output. In the world of literature, and in the visual arts, there has often been a direct reflection of faith in relation to art. In the ancient world, there were direct correlations between religion and such areas as law, medicine, science and politics. In some instances, these direct relationships remain. The law of marriage in Britain is still much influenced by theological considerations. Discussion of medical ethics often includes a religious input. Politics is affected by Christian traditions, with good and bad effects.

We have stressed the need for theology and the churches to build effective bridges to culture, against the anti-modern trends of much contemporary theology and practice. But of course not all accommodation to culture is good. For Christians, there can be a bridge only to link up with the basic human values at the centre of the Gospel – love, peace, justice, forgiveness and reconciliation. Inculturation which encourages and intensifies coercion, oppression, racial discrimination and the like is always wrong. As is often noted, churches which have practised apartheid have been perfect examples of inculturation of Christianity with evil. Studies of the social policies of the churches often show an alliance with reaction and uncharitable prejudice. It will be important to identify ambiguities in all such correlations. But the abuse does not take away the proper use.

There will always be the need for Christian communities to gather around centres of worship. Beyond this, they may seek to act as catalysts, as the salt of the earth. Within such a framework, the interaction of religion and culture, both at the margins and at the centres of cultures, becomes highly significant. It is impossible to bring support to the margins without adequate support from the centres. It is within this sort of vision that this chapter is developed. It is this transformative function, not necessarily turning everyone into traditional Christians, but offering a deeply Christian envelope for thought and praxis, which seems to offer a vital role for Christian theology and community in the future.

When we consider the influence of religion, and Christianity in particular, on culture and the arts, we think of the influence of religion on science and medicine in the ancient world, of Christianity on painting and prose up to the early twentieth century. Yet it would be hard to think of a decisive influence of Christianity on the humanities after say, 1950. By this time, the lawyers, historians and the like are doing what the natural scientists did earlier – producing their research without any reference to religion, though they may have private religious beliefs. Scientists may be Christian, but they will

not attempt to produce a Christian Science, nor lawyers
a Christian Law. (Exceptions may be found in some
traditional Catholic lawyers, such as John Finnis.) Even
within the theological disciplines themselves, there is a
huge stress on academic study within a professional guild,
without any reference to personal conviction or community engagement. After Auden and Eliot, it is hard to
think of major poets who struggle with religion in their
work. As for novelists, Walker Percy is often seen as the
last major Catholic novelist. Writers like Susan Howatch
or P. D. James can scarcely qualify as major literary
figures. At least in the European and North American
traditions, there appears to be a decline in that kind of
professional engagement with religion. There are
sociologists and philosophers of religion, but they are
themselves part of the academic religious guild. Where
writers do engage with religion, it is often in a highly
critical style – John Updike, Tom Wolfe, Umberto Eco.
In Europe, decline in engagement with religion seems to
follow the sharp decline in church attendance. Habermas
is here more typical than Gadamer. Only perhaps in music
is there still a notable existential interest in religion.

In black culture, there is perhaps still more engagement
than in white culture – one thinks of Alice Walker and
James Baldwin. But even here, the secularising influence
in the liberal arts is strong.

Yet there is this paradox, that there is still a strong
interest in religion in society. In North America, church-
going remains buoyant. Private religious feeling remains.
Theologians still write theology, often engaging with
culture. Where then is the cultural outlet for other
Christians and people of religious conviction?

If religion is to be a force for good in society – and
the major religions are all committed to such a vision –
then it is important that not only theologians should

be involved in trying to build bridges between religion and culture. What is needed is a reciprocity of dialogue and of effort to promote common human values. Part of the task of a Centre for Religion, Literature and the Arts is to examine such attempts at communicative action from all sides of the dialogue, and to encourage them to develop further in a diversity of fruitful directions. Different dimensions of culture will be involved in different ways, and it is not for any one of the dialogue partners to prescribe a methodology. At the same time, it may be possible to learn from analysis of praxis which kinds of dialogue are most likely to be fruitful, and which pitfalls are to be avoided.

There has been much concern in the liberation and emancipatory theologies for a close correlation of theology to praxis, in the name of love and justice. It will be interesting to see what response these movements produce in the wider culture beyond theological discussion. They come out of and encourage Christian communities engaged in struggle, and they invite to political and social action. Yet it will be strange if there is no corresponding engagement from other disciplines, for example from the arts. This may take the form of postmodern pluriformity, such as feminist theology in dialogue with women's studies and black theology with black studies. It has to be noted here that poetry and drama are themselves not as central to contemporary culture as they were in previous centuries. The impact of the mass media has created its own culture; and, though this has not neglected traditional art forms, it has led to a kind of marginalisation of them. Football, TV chat shows and soaps, pop music, and even the national lottery arguably have a much greater role in the shaping of culture. But it would be important in all areas of the humanities to provoke constructive engagement with theological themes on a much wider front, as Kierkegaard had an impact on Auden, or Anglican incarnational theology on Eliot. In Charles Taylor and Cornel West we see, largely implicitly, the beginnings of dialogue with late twentieth-century theology.

Seeking to balance an audit on the relation of Christianity to culture at the beginning of the twenty-first century, we may say that the fairly homogeneous pervasion of culture in Christendom is definitely over. We need not look back with nostalgia, for this culture raised as many questions as it solved for Christian faith – there was always the danger of unconscious and uncritical assimilation to inappropriate types of inculturation. Christian response over centuries to many central social issues, in such areas as crime and punishment, has on the whole been anything but exemplary. And in any case, Christendom was perhaps never as absolute as we occasionally imagine. It is a very long time since daily life, say in Britain, was run along the lines of a theocracy. Even in the time of Shakespeare, where poetry and drama are often saturated in religious imagery, Elizabethan business and diplomacy ran with religion *de facto* as often in the background as in the foreground of events. Religion, then and now, had much to do with how people spent their leisure moments, the quality time in which they might take stock and plan new strategies.

On the positive side of the account, the radical pluriformity of contemporary culture may provide new opportunities for imaginative initiatives at different levels in specific sectors of particular cultures, in fragments which may have an impact beyond their immediate location, as cultures overlap and interact in often unpredictable ways. These fragments may involve concentrated areas of Christian transformative symbolism, as often envisaged in Christian evangelical post-modernism.

But this is not the only possible alternative. They may also involve concrete and local instances of inter-cultural dialogue between faith and society of a more liberal sort. Such dialogue may involve the setting-out of unapologetic Christian perspectives. To describe such engagement, I am inclined to prefer the word *liberality*, to indicate a critical development beyond classical liberalism. Liberality involves generosity, centred on the generosity of God in Jesus Christ, but uncondi-tionally open to mutuality and reciprocity. To identify and pursue such avenues will involve both reference to areas of significant interaction in the present, and comparison with modes of interaction in the past. In this way, we may hope to arrive at guidelines for more effective intercultural dialogue between Christianity and society in the future. In seeking to examine response to the presence of God within the fragments of multi-cultural pluralism, we shall be pursuing further the discipline of theological intercultural hermeneutics.

Striking the appropriate balance between faith and culture is rarely easy. In the twentieth century, we saw this clearly in the world of Eliot and Auden. Both were highly critical of an easy accommodation with a tired liberalism. Faith provided a challenge and a place to stand *contra mundum*. Such an anti-modern stance can easily fall over into a defensive self-justification. But an effective interaction of faith and culture remains central to human flourishing.

A Role for Theology

Characteristic of the nineteenth century, of the modern age in theology, not least in the work of its founding father, F. D. E. Schleiermacher, was interdisciplinary study of theology and the humanities. The great theologians of the twentieth century were usually resolutely anti-modern, and their legacy in various editions of neo-orthodoxy has been an isolation of theology within its own bounds, accompanied by a marginalisation of the study of theology and the arts. The greatest of the anti-moderns, Barth and von Balthasar, were not unmindful of the humanities – Barth and Mozart, von Balthasar and aesthetics. Yet the trend has been to isolationism, or at best to an ideological makeover of the realm of culture, as for example in some of the writings of Lesslie Newbigin. On the credit side, there have been some modern systematic theologians who have not followed this trend – I think of David Tracy. But, on the whole, the field has been relegated to marginality. This has had profound consequences, both for the important task of dialogue between the disciplines, but also for the understanding of the nature of theological enquiry itself. Beyond this, it is highly instructive to reflect on the kinds of theological and ecclesiastical perspectives which have influenced the works of poets and playwrights, musicians, lawyers and scientists. Eliot and Auden, Mozart, Blackstone and Einstein – all were much affected by particular religious doctrines, and not always, we may think, for the better.

The ways in which Christian theology has interacted with different layers of culture and different disciplines are endless. Encounters which seem particularly fruitful to one Christian perspective will seem unfruitful to others. Most of the examples of interaction which I shall examine have had, in my view, both advantages and disadvantages for the development of engagement. This is inevitably the case. I shall attempt to suggest ways in which the advantages may be maximised and the disadvantages minimised. In this dialogue, as I see it, none of the partners has a privileged point of view. The theologian, the poet, the historian, the political scientist – all have contributions to make, and none has *the* master narrative which can encompass all else in an authoritative way. This is something which the theologians, at least, have been slow to learn. But the phenomenon also occurs in other forms of academic positivism, for example in the natural sciences.

Martha Nussbaum's *Cultivating Humanity* is a magnificent example of a series of studies which point to values at the heart of what it is to be human, through comparison and contrast in particular cultural contexts. It seems to me that Christian theology has an important contribution to that continuing task, and it is a contribution which is in serious need of articulation in the present. Nussbaum has been heavily criticised for her construal of human rights. It is arguable that she could have learned more from her critics and thereby strengthened her case. But what she has achieved has been deeply impressive.

Humane Praxis and Theological Partnership

The relation between social theology and the arts is a relationship of partnership. Christian theology is based on the divine love of God in Jesus Christ. Often its face has been of singularly loveless religion; but the abuse does not take away the proper use. Generosity even as an eschatological concept may have a considerable impact on the present. Theology as partnership should benefit from as well as contribute to the dialogue which is essential to human flourishing, and to the new creation which is God's purpose for all his creatures.

Liberation theology, it has sometimes been noted, has tended in recent years to lose some of its impetus. This is partly because it has often been ignored or subverted by conservative forces in the churches. But it may also be because the narrow base of oppression which is its great and enduring strength is also limited. Emancipatory theology needs to gain the confidence to participate in the widest human dialogue, reminding the human of the humane, in the name of God. In doing so, it should be able to gain new imagination and impetus, at a conceptual and also at a practical level. The crucified Christ at the centre of faith is also the risen Christ, the source of transformation, renewal and new horizons. This is not always possible in a situation of oppression. But the Christian hope is of the overcoming of evil by good.

A theology of humane praxis may seek to reimagine the basic contours of Christian doctrine, seeking to reflect a trace of the divine love in a contemporary way through its reshaping. To set this out in detail is always a major task, but to imagine some pointers should not be impossible.

Human language is inadequate to give us anything like a technical description of God. Yet there is the phenomenon of faith, which considers that in building up a cumulative case for belief in God it is responding to a source of meaning and loving purpose in the universe. Out of fragments of data, experience and interpretation, faith has developed as a community tradition, a tradition with many gaps and disjunctions, in Christianity and in the major world religions.

God is neither the patriarchal figure of the Hebrew Bible nor the kyriarchal figure of Christian tradition nor the mirror-image opposite of these. God includes relationship in Godself. The imagery of incarnation and trinity, through the Spirit of the crucified and risen Christ, reflects the concretion of this relationship. God cares about his creatures, and is the source of all generosity. God cares as humans care, as mothers, fathers, relatives and friends care. None of these images is privileged or excluded. But his care is perfect.

As a caring God, God thinks of his creatures' welfare and acts on their behalf. God is constantly active in creation, though not always able to act directly. God rejoices when they rejoice and suffers when they suffer. God is unable to prevent premature or tragic human death, but he brings eschatological salvation to all creation. God is concerned for the welfare of human society, as well as for non-human creatures and the cosmic environment. Divine love instantiates mutuality, reciprocity and inclusiveness. It creates forgiveness and reconciliation and the mending of brokenness. It includes justice and peace. Each of these spheres calls for infinite effort and infinite patience.

Divine love restores the damaged and injured to new creation by solidarity and unconditional identification. That is the spontaneity of grace, which is at once the great asset and the great judgment upon the community of those who believe. God's action leads towards a goal of new creation, of participation in the perfect relationship of the divine society. Because this is a society of love, peace and justice, it is the signal of direction to which all our social life is invited to move.

Praxis

Perhaps most commonly, occasions of solidarity and identification are tied in our contemporary society to more or less absolute poverty:

There is a light that never goes out. They emerge from the stairway into the darkness of the street. Some of them move in a jerky, manic way; noisy and exuberant. Others cruise along silently, like ghosts, hurting inside, yet fearful of the imminence of even greater pain and discomfort. Their destination is a pub which seems to prop up a crumbling tenement set on a side-street between Easter Road and Leith Walk. This street has missed out on the stone-cleaning process its neighbours have enjoyed and the building is the sooty-stone colour of a forty-a-day man's lungs. The night is so dark that it is difficult to establish the outline of the tenement against the sky. It can only be defined through an isolated light glaring from a top floor window or the luminous street-lamp jutting from its side.

. . .

'Come hame wi us for a while Danny. Nae drugs or any-thing. Ah dinnae want tae be ooan ma ain now, Danny. Ken whit ah'm sayin.' Alison looks at him tensely, tearfully, as they lurch along the street. Spud nods, he thinks he knows what she is saying, because he doesn't want to be alone either. He never can be quite sure, though, never ever quite sure.

(Irvine Welsh, *Trainspotting*, pp. 262, 272)

There is the challenge.

Till you get to a stage which is already today's, but may be more tomorrow's, where you have an anthropological type you might call the self-made nitwit, the smart semi-educated nonentity, moneyed without being mannered, with an anything-that-sells-is-good mentality, who thinks values are made on the stock exchange, who's never without lap-top and portable and who, being proud of his Scottish identity, gets married in a kilt.

Kenneth White, from *The Consignia Lecture* 2001

9

'Clyde-built, Edinburgh-managed'

Voice and Place in Scottish Culture

Willy Slavin

Ane Satyre of the Thrie Estaitis provided in 1540 a severe critique of the Scots establishment of king, parliament and church from the point of view of an ordinary person, John the Commonweal. Over the following three centuries, Scotland, remarkably for a European nation, saw all three of these institutions effectively emasculated as representative of Scotland. A nation without state institutions is an anomaly. Daiches describes the survival of a national culture in Scotland as paradoxical.

Briefly: in 1603, the King of Scots accepted an invitation to go to London and become the King of England. In 1707, the members of the Scottish parliament voted to join the English parliament. In 1843, the Kirk split itself in two, with half conforming to the unionist establishment and the other half effectively denying validity to the politics of earthly nationality.

As a result, Scotland lost its internal coherence. In different parts of Scotland, quite different voices are heard. *North Britain* is centred on Edinburgh. The fact that there is relatively little movement to it from the rest of the country is one indicator that it doesn't really function as a national capital. Rather, it has been a colonial outpost of London, the capital of Britain. The *West of Scotland* is based around the Clyde, facing the Atlantic and open to influences from the Gaelic Highlands and Islands, from Ireland and from the Americas. Edinburgh as the administrative centre and Glasgow as the industrial base have served as major magnets for cultural activity in Scotland. However, it needs to be remembered that there are other places with different voices such as the *North-East*, not only guardian of a vigorous ballad tradition but also home of the couthie *Sunday Post*.

In North Britain, under sustained pressure from the Scottish Enlightenment, a rational deism became the prevailing religious orthodoxy. The threat of French revolutionary fervour was met with a Presbyterian-ordered liberal morality. Edinburgh found a certain integrity by taking on the respectability of Scott's novels, though it remained the city of Jekyll and Hyde (to say nothing of *Trainspotting*). In the twentieth century, the liberal political consensus was challenged by Irish independence which stimulated a debate between unionism and nationalism. From this emerged the Scottish National Party. The current aggregation (rather than combination) of unionist and nationalist sentiment is neatly illustrated each year by the Edinburgh International Festival. From all over the world, tourists pour into Britain's most beautiful city. Its financial capital has permitted it to hoard jealously Scotland's cultural heritage. Yet contemporary Scottish artists regularly complain that little opportunity is given to them to produce their wares, and they dismiss the Festival as Brigadoonery and Balmorality.

In the West of Scotland, unmoderated Calvinism and ultramontane Catholicism were both savaged by industrial materialism. Glasgow gave birth to the archetypal

Scot – the engineer. The industrialisation of the Clyde basin was based on an alliance of the middle class with a skilled working class, both of which were significantly non-conformist in their church affiliation. In addition, the Second City of the Empire required an enormous labouring pool which left many destitute and prey to despair. This was resisted by diverse movements. Checkland calls Glasgow *the city of the social gospel.* It gave a very significant input into the early success of the (British) Labour Party. And there were more radical voices, such as those heard in the 1915 women's rent strike with its echoes of Celtic matriarchy. In 1919, London sent tanks to Glasgow, fearing Bolshevik revolution. If today, as the Tourist Office proclaims, Glasgow Smiles Better, it is often through gritted teeth. The revived historical centre is still ringed by post-war housing estates which Billy Connolly dubbed '*deserts wi' windaes*'.

Eventually Westminster, in alliance with municipal Labour, succeeded in managing Scotland, as Andrew Marr puts it, with *a tawse of iron.* The recovery of the Stone of Destiny by some nationalists was generally regarded as a mere jape, akin to putting a tack on the headmaster's chair. The giving of a Scottish title to the new queen's Greek-born husband was taken no more seriously. As England's first and most successful colonials, apparently this was thought an indulgence that the Scots could be afforded. Nevertheless, the paradox remained. On either side of the border, villagers separated from each other by a few fields spoke with different voices. Langholm is not Longtown.

Edwin Muir identified a Scot as *someone who thinks in English but feels like a Scot.* Hugh MacDiarmid said: *I'm a Scot wha blindly follows auld Scottish instincts.* Tom Leonard deliberately used Scottish vernacular as a way of dissociating himself from the Establishment, a tactic now common among contemporary writers in Scotland. This offers recognition of Scots *not as a dialect but as a different way of speaking*. And, although the voices vary according to different parts of the country, they have in common something distinct from English voices.

To date, the First Minister remains uncrowned. Indifference to the House of Windsor, it would seem, is not equivalent to republican sentiment. It is still not clear whether the restoration of the parliament in itself will be enough to resolve the *Caledonian antisyzygy*. However, it should be said that the question of whether national emancipation is a subject worthy of faith is clearly a task for any social theology calling itself Scottish. It is intriguing that in Scotland there is not an overabundance of religious writing. So it is not surprising that the question of independence has not provoked much explicit religious commentary. Perhaps there is the suspicion that Presbyterianism, which would seem tailor-made for Scottish independence, has been hijacked long since by unionism. In general, it could be said that in the arts theological interest has been gradually muffled, not to say finally strangled, in our own time. And yet there is evidence that many of the voices that are most characteristic of Scotland include dimensions that are open to a wider epiphany.

The excerpts of poetry and prose in this book are examples of such voices – quotations intended to illustrate the concerns of John and Jean Commonweal. They come from experiences common to ordinary people in this country. Whatever form Scotland's political institutions take in the future, they will only acquire coherence by taking account also of what is said and sung, played and painted across the nation. Taken as a whole, these quotations may be regarded as coming from what has been called the voices of *the prodigal children of Christianity*. This is not to suggest either that the authors have all abandoned the faith of their fathers and mothers or, on the other hand, that they would all accept a religious appellation. It is to propose, rather, that among the commonalities of voices identified as Scottish there is explicit talk about justice, peace and the integrity of creation.

Something is green in the house
of a sudden:
all morning I finger the windows
revealing the moisture,
        the heartbeat that rises through stone,

and later, in the stillness after Mass,
I guess what it might have been
to discover the tomb:
the empty linen printed with a stain

of presence, like a broken chrysalid,
where something has struggled loose,
through remembrance and pain,
and the angel, a handsbreadth away,
in the blood-scented shade,
a breathless, impossible being, diverting my gaze,
from that which is risen, the living unnameable God.

                    John Burnside, from *The Resurrection*

Part IV

Doing Social Theology: Church Ways of Working

Two chapters investigating respectively the Catholic Church and the Church of Scotland are offered here as means of introduction and challenge rather than as conclusion on the churches' doing of social theology in Scotland today. Whether through their public statements or work on the ground, they represent but a part of the Scottish churches' context.

This said, there is certainly a good deal of interest both in the substance and impact (or not) of the social theological work here described. Within the Catholic Church, there is a history of magisterial statements alongside the influence of community experience, at home and abroad, which in Scotland could be said to influence the formulations of so-called 'social teaching' and involvement in issues of social justice. It is noted that there is room for an extension of what might be contributed, both in academic terms and through avenues of popular participation; but a leading question is around the helpfulness or not of statements from 'on high' – in the recent Scottish context not least where there has been a word spoken 'from' church 'to' nation. As an ecclesiological question, this has a significance beyond matters of church order; it goes apart from issues of episcopal or presbyterial government. This emerges clearly in Chapter 11, which deals with the work of the General Assembly (national) committees of the Church of Scotland. Though there may be differing theological starting points within the one church and its structures, as long as there are assumptions that the few may act and speak for the many, there is a risk of disconnections and lack of take-up of the social-justice agenda within the wider life of the church. This is not an unrecognised problem, but it nevertheless awaits satisfactory solutions – probably ecumenically. The churches may indeed have important words and acts of witness to offer those outside the fold, but the task of translating and 'incarnating' the life of Christ addresses equally those within the churches themselves.

Chapters 12–14, on the work and witness of the Evangelical Alliance, the Iona Community and the European Ecumenical Commission on Church and Society (EECCS), offer wider reflections on what might be described as a focused layering of church life – outside denominational limits and involving a commitment to both personal and communal discipline and institutional dialogue in the doing of social theology (though there would be a reticence about the possibly 'grandiose' tones of that term). The Evangelical Alliance challenges its cross-denominational supporters to embrace and develop the great Evangelical tradition of a biblically rooted social concern in a fresh commitment to social transformation in the new Scottish political context. Those who belong to the Iona Community or come into a visiting contact with its core people are invited into a solid model of participation and belonging that looks always to break out of being too self-regarding. It is not a perfect model, in that there is a vital principle of *semper reformanda* (always needing to be reformed), but in its beckoning into community-making it exemplifies a true challenge. And finally, in a local Scottish context where the wider European dimension is of growing importance, the work of EECCS offers a model of dialogue with the European institutions that pursues a theology of insistence as the basis of the church's mission. It reminds us in closing that, in the twenty-first century, every local contextual theology must engage with the emerging global order. This whole collection of essays represents work in progress in an unfinished task and a changing world but always in the light of the Gospel.

10

The Role of Catholic Social Teaching in Scotland Today

Gerard R. Hand

How Catholics in Scotland see themselves and how others see them has been a cause of some study in the last few years. This has occurred as Catholics identify themselves more fully as Scottish, and as they develop their identity in a changing Scotland. One of the challenges helping the Catholic Church to grow is how it should establish its specific contribution to the common good of the nation. It isn't the purpose of this chapter to discuss the various meanings of 'Church', but it is sufficient to note, that as in any writing of this type, we will touch on different meanings, ranging from the Christian responding to Christ's call in the workplace to the bishops issuing a pastoral letter. I will try to identify how Catholic social teaching affects various parts of the Catholic Church institutionally, and also how lay Catholics in their work and in society display the influence of social teaching. How Catholic social teaching affects other churches and people in society is more than this chapter can deal with, other than in a most impressionistic way.

Centralisation might be how many would want to start describing power in the Catholic Church. There are elements of truth in this, but it is equally important to realise that the eight bishops and dioceses in Scotland are independent of one another, and find their essential unity in the unity they share with the college of bishops with the Pope at its head. Although Cardinal Winning was called head of the Catholic Church in Scotland by the press, strictly speaking he was president of the hierarchy. It is possible for the hierarchy to elect another bishop as president. The concept of the national hierarchy has developed since the Second Vatican Council, but in fact is still in very early days. This means that the national committees are not strong, and in many ways the dioceses go their own way. This makes a common voice difficult to achieve on an institutional basis, never mind trying to achieve a common voice of all Catholics. One of the challenges facing the church is, while preserving the theological integrity of the diocese, to implement the basic values of Catholic social teaching in its methods of organisation. Some important developments have taken place, but more has to be done.

There has been an explosion of books on Catholic social teaching, for example *Our Best Kept Secret*, which shows a growing awareness of social teaching as a theological source. There is a risk involved in this, in that it could be interpreted almost as rules that can be applied and solutions found. Within the Catholic concept of magisterium – the teaching authority of the church – social teaching, like other church teaching, is seen as a development and application of the church's reflection and experience of the Gospel. It is related in some way to Revelation. There has been theological discussion as to whether the appropriate terminology is 'social doctrine'[1] or 'social teaching', but social teaching seems to be preferred because it presents a less sure vision in a very complex and changing world.

The term 'social teaching' stems from the encyclical *Rerum Novarum* of 1890. It was an attack on unbridled capitalism, but was still reflecting a relatively conservative social view. It was however the foundation of Catholic social teaching, which has been developing in its understanding of society since. The three main values of the teaching are seen as:

- the dignity of the person
- the solidarity of various parts of society
- the idea of subsidiarity, meaning authority being exercised at an appropriate level.

Historical Background of Social Involvement

Catholics before the Irish immigration were relatively few in number, and were mainly in the north of Scotland. They tended to keep a fairly low profile. With the coming of industrialisation, and with the internal immigration of Scottish Catholics and Irish immigration, that profile grew, particularly within central Scotland. The community was intent on survival, and banded together to develop and maintain an identity, though there were serious divisions within it. There was an alliance between a largely working-class population and some Scottish aristocrats and gentry who subsidised a substantial amount of church-building. The 'pennies of the poor' as the foundation of the development of the Catholic Church in Scotland was only partially true.[2]

Some of the Catholic immigrants coming into industrial work in central Scotland were a threat to some of the more organised workers in terms of the conditions that they were prepared to work in, but were not particularly different from other internal immigrant workers. Recent research that has shown some social and political involvement by Irish immigrant workers challenges the myth that the Irish immigrants were all strike-breakers and held back the development of organised labour.[3]

In the twentieth century, various groups and associations tried to develop the involvement of the Catholic Church in the society of the time. Part of the intention was to combat communism, but there was also a desire to contribute to a renewed world order which would combat unbridled capitalism. This reflected much of the papal social teaching of the twentieth century which saw capitalism as a major enemy.[4] Groups such as the Young Christian Workers, based on the see–judge–act model, groups associated with Plater College, and the Catholic Social Evidence Guild, maintained some level of consciousness that Catholics should be trying to help develop social conditions on Christian principles.[5] A substantial number of these groups tended in practice to be study groups rather than action groups. They did produce, however, people who were socially aware and concerned about justice in society.

The social conditions that many Catholics lived in produced other people who became active in unions and political parties (especially latterly, in the Labour Party). I am not clear what the relationship was between these people and the social teaching groups, but there was some crossover between them. Also we see here the question of whether Catholic social teaching is the root and inspiration of social action or is a means of encouraging and challenging Catholics who have already embarked on political action. It seems to me that in Scotland it has carried out both functions. John Wheatley is someone who represented both tendencies.

The Second Vatican Council, 1962–5

The Second Vatican Council happened as Catholics in Scotland were beginning to feel more secure in the country and were entering different levels of the nation's life. It called on Catholics to relate to the world and to learn from the world, as it made clear that the basic call of the baptised was to live out their calling in the work-place and the home. The paradox is that, while that was a fundamental thrust of the council documents, the encouragement of the laity to be more involved in the pastoral and institutional life of the church has led numerically to many more people being involved pastorally (eucharistic ministers, readers, bereavement groups, pastoral councils) and to a limited increase in the amount of people being involved in the social-justice side of the church's activities. To say that, of course, does not tackle the question of whether the Catholic population today is more or less politically and socially aware than it was forty years ago.

Catholics in Scotland Today

Catholics now clearly identify themselves as Scots and feel they belong in Scotland. Recent discussion has dwelt on whether discrimination still exists. That is still an open question, but there is little doubt that the situation of acceptance has changed in recent years.

Professor McCrone's work shows that Catholics, surprisingly for some, tend to be on the left with regard to most social issues, with the exception of abortion.[6] Why that should be is not clear, but we may look to the poorer social conditions in which the present generation of middle-aged Catholics grew up and perhaps also to the memory of being a discriminated-against immigrant minority. In the context of the latter point, it is important to remember that the Irish are not the only immigrant group in Scottish Catholics, although they are the largest. We may also look to the influence of the Catholic education system, Missio and SCIAF, knowledge of and contact with church in different parts of the world, and the ecumenical contacts in Scotland.

As the Catholic population established itself in Scotland, there was a sense of service, an emphasis on education and on vocations like doctors, priests and teachers, which was rooted in the values of the Gospel as well as being the result of a minority and immigrant experience.

As part of a population influenced negatively by Thatcherism, Catholics in general seem to be open to political and social questions being part of the church's agenda. The question for the institutional church is how broad is its approach, and whether a *perceived* narrowness of approach might not weaken the important counter-cultural things it has to say and do.

Catholic Social Teaching in Scotland

Social teaching is not only what can be identified in an academic sense as social teaching. We have, however, to take into account that the Catholic Church in Scotland has not been able to develop a Catholic institute or foundation that would be able to provide the research base for substantial locally based work, and so on the academic level it has not contributed what it might have.

Papal social teaching has been influential in Scotland. The key work of Pope Paul VI was important in helping people see the relationship of the personal and structural, as was his Decree on Evangelisation. The teachings of John Paul II, for example on work, international and national community, and areas of moral responsibility, have challenged Catholics in Scotland to think and live out what the dignity of the person means in the various levels of community that they live in today. Although there would be basic goodwill towards his social teaching, there would be ongoing discussion regarding both the content and the method of his social teaching, particularly as he would tend towards calling the latter 'social doctrine', a term which some would feel too close to attempting dogmatic statements in political and social affairs.

Other international teachings such as the Medellin and Puebla conferences, the US bishops' letters on nuclear weapons and on the economy, and the English and Welsh bishops' *The Common Good*, have been studied and reflected on within a Scottish context.[7] The US bishops' letter on the economy has been appreciated for its collaborative method of being prepared and written as well as its content.

The Catholic Bishops' Conference of Scotland has produced a variety of teachings: the 1982 pastoral letter on nuclear weapons and the 1987 statement on Trident, the statements on South Africa, the statements on women, and the various statements associated with the January World Day of Prayer for Peace. These have been produced in a variety of ways, some collaboratively with the Justice and Peace Commission and some more directly from the conference. A particular concern grew as the press talked about Cardinal Winning as the head of the Catholic Church in Scotland, and gave great weight to his statements, whether they approved of them or not. Cardinal Winning was the President of the Bishops' Conference and could make statements on its behalf, but not as head of the church in Scotland (which he did not claim to be). In contrast with papal social teaching, of which the background, composition and history, revision and publication are usually well documented, the background of statements coming from the Bishops' Conference, individual bishops, commissions or committees is not always clear. This, along with the late Cardinal Winning's willingness to speak out on many social issues, made him a natural focus for Catholics and the media. Catholic teaching at any level has to be evaluated as to how the truth is perceived within it, what is the authority of the source, and the method of preparation.

Archbishop O'Brien has produced several letters which give a statement and provide a means for parish groups to reflect and act on the issues contained in the letters. Examples of this are (1) his 1987 letter on poverty and justice sparked off by his visit to El Salvador and the assassination of Herbor Anaya, a leading human-rights activist, and (2) the letter in 2000 on the visit of Bishop Ruiz of Chiapas on the twentieth anniversary of the assassination of Archbishop Romero. These letters try to help people reflect on injustice in Scotland in the light of situations of injustice abroad. This would reflect former SCIAF worker John Dornan's report from El Salvador of a group of people who said the best thing the people of Scotland could do for them was to work for justice in Scotland.

The Scottish Teaching in Practice

The Scottish Catholic Justice and Peace Commission developed in the 1980s to challenge the church and help it live out the Gospel values of justice and peace. The word order of the title was seen to be important, reflecting the belief that there can be no true peace without justice. Unlike many other countries' commissions, the Scottish one is not separate from the network of Justice and Peace groups. The value of this is that there is a network which can try to take on some of the challenges of justice and which can feed back concerns. Disadvantages are that the work can be too multifaceted, with the attendant difficulty of applying the weight of the church behind an issue, and that there are not enough resources for adequate research. The *Justice and Peace* magazine does provide on an ecumenical basis a platform for the development of justice issues both theoretically and practically.

A key gain over the years of the work of the Commission, in conjunction with other influences, is that where at times in the past justice and peace issues and people were seen to be on the periphery of the church's life, they are now seen to be much more central. Whether the perception is backed up in practice is a different matter. Social teaching overall has been experienced as an inspiration and challenge, and as a means of evaluating work and causes which people instinctively commit to.

Other Ways by which Catholics are Influenced by Social Teaching

The Scottish Catholic International Aid Fund (SCIAF) and Missio are institutions of the church; but, in reflecting on their influence in the implementation of social teaching, we have to see that there are different models of membership, of the church, and of SCIAF and Missio, legitimately at work.

SCIAF is the church in different ways. It is also many things: it is staff in an office in Glasgow; it is the people who are on their mailing lists; it is the people in the pews who contribute financially and identify with SCIAF; it is the lapsed Catholics who feel an empathy with

SCIAF; it is the groups of people who work at SCIAF's campaigns reaching out beyond the confines of the Catholic church in Scotland; it is the people of other denominations and faiths who have been touched by SCIAF.

SCIAF has provided practical assistance to many projects; but, in trying to encourage Catholics to think through what development means, it has also helped some of them to think through what development in Scotland is. By bringing in partners from overseas, they have exposed parishes and groups to the challenge from the partners that the church should be about justice, not simply giving money. Through its work of education, SCIAF has helped people appreciate that there is such a thing as Catholic social teaching. In this context, it is likely that SCIAF's work over the years has been influential in the fact that Catholics tend to the left sociologically in justice and development issues, both at home and abroad.

Missio is an international organisation of the church to facilitate its work in helping young churches to develop and the Gospel to be preached. It is an office in Rome. It helps distribute financial help to young churches. It is also, however, a focus of missionary awareness among Catholics in Scotland. By being exposed to the work of Missio and to the experiences of missionaries, and to the knowledge that the Catholic Church in other countries operates in different conditions and in different ways, at least some Catholics have been able to imagine different ways of being church in Scotland. They have also been challenged to accept that people in other countries are of equal dignity with them.

Renewal and training programmes are very important. Courses such as the Craighead Faith and Life Course and the Working for Change programme, as well as a number of renewal programmes or Lenten programmes used by various dioceses, have had substantial elements of social teaching within them. This has meant that there has been a move from 'J&P' training to church training (for example pastoral councils) which is based on the three basic social teaching values of dignity, solidarity and subsidiarity. This is helping a gradual and slow shift in consciousness as to what the church is about in terms of its working for the transformation of society as well as personal conversion.

The communitarian philosophy of the partnership of family, school and parish has had some influence on developing a sense of community. Whether that sense can survive the individualism of the modern period remains to be seen, but it is reasonable to suppose that the school system has had an influence on the sociological observations we have already seen. Integral to the school system has been the influence of the SCIAF and Missio campaigns, and so the young people from Primary 1 onwards have been exposed to the social-justice teaching of the church in the ethos of the school, and in the specific RE teaching that develops attitudes referring to social justice.

It is at least arguable that the fact of living in parish communities and diocesan communities, no matter how difficult they are to define, helps Catholics resist, perhaps on a subconscious level, the excessive individualism of modern society. That might be too optimistic, but at least it may be that the knowledge that we are called to live in community is a challenge to the conscience of people deeply influenced by a society that struggles with community. Exposure to the Word of God and participation in the celebration of the Eucharist, both interpreted in the light of social teaching, which in turn comes from them, sensitises people (even if only in part) to the demands of justice.[8]

Challenges from within
the Social Teaching

Catholic social teaching can be a vague tag which people can hide behind to do what they were going to do anyway. It can also be the 'hidden secret' which some want to keep hidden, because of the challenge it contains. It does, however, when taken fully and seriously, challenge the negative aspects of the positive value of Catholics feeling accepted in society, namely the temptation not to accept the challenge to be willing to stand up for a different society.

To do that, the institutional church will have to evaluate itself within the perspectives of social teaching. This will be challenging, but also it will be liberating. True authority and collaboration give rise to hope rather than despair.

Catholics are active in many levels of society, but whether there has been a sufficient commitment on a civic level, both local and national, from local parishes and dioceses is doubtful. Resources were not devoted to the Scottish Convention or, as far as can be seen, to the Civic Forum. Part of the reason for that is that the Catholic church, for sometimes good theological reasons, does not organise easily on a national level.

The difference in structures within the churches hinders both the definition and practice of what ecumenical activity in developing social thinking and practice actually can mean. The Catholic Church, like the other churches, is called to develop its sense of how there can be a greater sense of common planning and not what can very often be the case in practice of one church asking others to join in its plans. ACTS is an attempt to overcome this flaw, but it seems at the moment that both ACTS and the individual churches need to assess the blocks to the common planning that leads to common activity. That is true both locally and nationally.

Conclusion

Catholic social teaching is a challenge of the Gospel which, as more and more people in Scotland are coming to see, has to convert the structures of society at the same time as individuals are converted. It is also a challenge to the church to keep struggling for justice within itself, as well as in the society in which it lives.

Notes

1. P. Hebblethwaite, 'The Popes and Politics', in *Official Catholic Social Teaching*, ed. Curran and McCormick, Paulist Press, 1986.

2. B. Aspinwall, 'Faith of Our Fathers Living Still: The Time Warp or Woof! Woof!', in *Scotland's Shame?*, ed. T. M. Devine, Mainstream, 2000, p. 110.

3. J. F. McCaffrey, 'Irish Issues in the Nineteenth and Twentieth Century: Radicalism in a Scottish Context', in *Irish Immigrants and Scottish Society in the Nineteenth and Twentieth Centuries*, ed. T. M. Devine, John Donald, 1991, p. 125. T. M. Devine, *The Scottish Nation*, Penguin, 1999, p. 490.

4. D. Dorr, *Option for the Poor*, Gill & Macmillan, 1992, p. 94.

5. T. A. Fitzpatrick, 'The Catholic Social Guild: Fr. Leo O'Hea, S.J. (1881–1976), and the West of Scotland Connection', *Innes Review* (Autumn 1999), pp. 127–38.

6. D. McCrone, 'Catholics in Scotland: a sociological view', in *Catholicism and the Future of Scotland*, Occasional Paper No. 39, CTPI, Edinburgh, 1997.

7. US Bishops, *Building Economic Justice*, United States Catholic Conference, 1986.

8. G. R. Hand, 'Church and Local Community', in *Open House*, March 1999, pp. 4–5.

On the rare occasions when I (still) hear that Calvinism is a core element in Scottish identity, I not only have to stifle a yawn but also stop myself from laughing, reflecting on my own extraction. Though exposed to the distasteful rigours and the thoughtless philistinism of a well-known Glasgow Jesuit school, I cannot regret all the aspects of a Catholic upbringing. Old enough to have regularly attended mass in Latin, I licked my fingertip and leafed through the thin pages of a bilingual missal with fascination. I have loved parallel texts ever since. Visiting Italy for the first time aged 15, religious ritual and church furnishing were unremarkably familiar. Renaissance altarpieces never appeared foreign to me, and I immediately developed a passion for angels which is yet to abandon me. When this dangerously cosmopolitan and international Catholicism is contrasted with the sturdy virtues of a national reformed church peculiar only to this country and productive of a rugged Scottish character, all I can do is shrug my shoulder. They expect that I should envy monochrome conformity (as if the Calvinists had ever been able to agree among themselves!). They will be disappointed.

Christopher Whyte, from *Across the Water*

Social Theology in the Church of Scotland

David Sinclair

The Church of Scotland, catholic and reformed, established and free, approaches social theology in its national
structures through the General Assembly and its committee system, in particular in the work of the Church
and Nation Committee. The Board of Social Responsibility can also lay claim to some input to this work;
but, as will be shown later, much of its work can be
seen as relating to the relationship of the church to
society, rather than an examination of society itself.
Differences of approach can be traced back to the influence of different strands brought together in one church
in 1929, that of the national church and that of the Free
Church.

In recent years, however, the influence of liberation
theology has been felt even in these northern climes,
an influence which puts much emphasis on analysing
not only what we see but the position of our seeing.
It sets us in our context, not only locally but also
nationally and globally. This then asks the question of
who are best placed to see the reality of what is going
on; the answer for liberationism being that those on
the underside of society and history can see in a way
which others cannot. Through the continuing contact

with the world church provided, among others, by the Board of World Mission, this perspective can be seen in recent times to have informed not only the work of both bodies mentioned so far but also the Board of National Mission in its Urban Priority Areas Committee, its Priority Areas Fund and the work towards an ecumenical Scottish Churches Community Development Fund. We will therefore argue that, while there is much that leads to differing emphases, there is a growing body of experience and theological reflection which is unifying, bringing the work of these different traditions together and resulting, among other things, in groups such as the Scottish Churches Social Inclusion Network.

More and more, the church is eschewing the temptation to speak from 'on high', preferring a more earthed, contextual and incarnational theology. It also seeks to work with others, including those in other churches, far more often than it once did. The report to the 2000 General Assembly said:

> Today we require a more nuanced and complex understanding of the church's social role. It increasingly has to act in partnership with other churches and with various social groups, bodies and agencies. Its political witness is often most effective when such partnerships are formed around particular issues, such as Jubilee 2000.

There are, of course, those within the Church of Scotland and some in other Christian denominations who would wish that the church spoke rather more often from 'on high'. Among those consulted in the preparation of this work was at least one such voice bewailing the fact that the Church of Scotland does not speak for all the churches as, at least in relation to Westminster, it has the legal right to do.

The Church and Nation Committee

Following the third report, in 1919, of the special commission looking into the life of the Church of Scotland,
the General Assembly accepted its recommendation that
a committee on national life be set up to be 'the voice
and the handmaid' of the church. It was and is to speak
on any matter in the life of the nation which has moral
or spiritual implications, a definition and a job description which excludes very little. It has therefore
spoken on many subjects over the time of its existence,
advising the General Assembly, keeping the church
informed and involved in the life of the nation. Although
it has gone through many conveners in its time and many
more changes in membership, the committee has maintained its existence as the committee on national life of
a national church. That is to say that it has consistently
taken the view that it is possible to speak to church and
to nation at the same time. Its concern has never been
simply for the well-being of the church but that of the
nation; and, when faced with a choice, it will still
advocate what is best for the nation as a whole, even if
that were to conflict with what is best for the church.

A recent example of this (1999) is the debate over
reform of the House of Lords. The Church of Scotland
was asked to respond to the Royal Commission specifically on the question of whether religious representation
in a reformed second chamber should be widened to
include people from the Church of Scotland and others.
The Church and Nation Committee insisted on asking
first: what kind of second chamber is best for the nation?
It has been consistently difficult to persuade politicians
of the importance for the church of this question, and to
persuade them that the question of the church's direct
involvement is, for the church, secondary.

Is this a hangover of a mistaken Constantinianism, a throwback to an imagined golden age of Christendom? Or is it a refusal of self-interest, a voluntary assumption of responsibility, which is at its heart profoundly theological? These are questions to do with what it means to be a 'national' church, with whether a nation can be ministered to almost in spite of itself, with the ability of the community of faith to carry a vision of the kingdom of God on behalf of the community at large. They are also questions which go straight to the heart of the relationship of religion to politics, with how a church can presume to comment on the life of the nation and with what authority it does that. They are, finally, questions which are inherited from the Baillie Commission of the Second World War, a commission which provided a way of working which has endured and a set of questions which require continually to be revisited.[1]

The Baillie Commission recognised the extent to which Christianity as the presumed framework for living and thinking in Scotland was declining and that secularism was the setting for mission, public affairs and moral commitment. It therefore realised that communication with a secular society would have to be carried out on a common moral ground. The question of how to speak within a pluralist context remains for the church today. The Baillie Commission spoke of the needs of the poor and the oppressed as being central concerns for the church. But it left with future generations the question of finding a way of speaking *with* rather than *for* or *at* the poor and the oppressed. Baillie used the middle-axiom approach to social ethics which seeks to build consensus, but it left the question for the church of how to work when consensus is not possible.[2]

The Church and Nation Committee struggles with these questions on an issue-by-issue basis rather than by a systematised attempt at theory development. Thus, in the Constitutional Convention and the Scottish Land Reform Convention, the attempt is made to work with those who are interested in a particular issue whether or not the same people could be worked with on other issues. Pluralism is recognised in practice, and common ground is marked out. These continuing conversations with others on specific issues evidence a dialectical approach to work in and with the wider society. Perhaps, however, the Committee has not always been clear enough about the theological grounding for working as it does. Andrew McLellan, a previous convener, said this:

> Questions about middle axioms, about contextual theological analysis, about how we do social thinking in the church hardly have an opportunity to feature on the committee's agenda ... there is not for the committee an agreed and sustained body of theological principle by which it is able to be helped and to help the church.[3]

Speaking with the poor is something the Committee has in the past tried to achieve but has found difficult. It has recognised the success of Church Action on Poverty (CAP) in its hearings and Bob Holman in his encouragement of people with experience of poverty to write about it; and in November 1999 it learnt with interest of the All-Party Committee on Poverty in the House of Commons, chaired by Ernie Ross MP, and its experiments at involvement of those with direct experience of living on or below the breadline. The Committee itself has still to develop patterns of working which match these.

Speaking when there is no consensus can be seen to have changed in recent years within the work of the Church and Nation Committee. The most obvious example would be the difference in approach between what was said at the time of the Gulf War in 1991 and at the time of the NATO intervention in Kosovo and Serbia in 1999. In 1991, the tone was much more critical, fearful that moral high ground was being claimed by those who were principally interested in economic and political hegemony. In other words, even though a consensus was not possible, the Committee chose to speak 'a word of truth to power' to speak as prophetically as possible, knowing that truth is neither measured in numbers nor arrived at as a compromise. In 1999, the tone was more measured. The Committee made every effort to hold together those who saw no good and a great deal of evil coming from the bombing, and those who wanted 'something done' about the atrocities being reported daily from the Kosovan border. There were those in the General Assembly who remarked on this difference, seeing political allegiance or a loss of nerve as the underlying reasons. There were certainly differences in the conflict, but perhaps the real difference was that to be found in the *contextual community*.

The importance of community is a key to all the social theology of the church. It can be seen to lie behind some of the differences of emphasis as well as some of the signs of convergence. There is an ecclesiological issue here which needs to be explored because in that exploration is to be found much which can be of help in a more general understanding.

The Church and Nation Committee produced reports in 1996 and 1997 on, respectively, 'Poverty and Community Development' and 'Community Development: What Hope for the Poor?' But it is to a slightly earlier report that we must look for a rounded analysis of the concept of community itself. In 1993, the Committee produced a report on 'The Importance of Community'. In this, it stated:

The church's role as co-creator and nurturer of community, under God, of all God's people is crucial for the well-being of society as a whole, particularly when symptoms of the breakdown of community abound . . . Ideal community derives from the ultimate community traditionally seen in the triune God whose mark is infinite love. Community must therefore be marked by love, characterised by caring, tolerance, understanding, forgiveness and acceptance in the image of divine love, and though mankind is capable of building only provisional community such building takes place in anticipation of perfect community, the Kingdom of God.

Within such an anticipation, the report looked at three kinds of community – that of the family, the church and society. The family was held to be the place where we learn (or ought to learn) what community is (or ought to be), a place of mutual valuing, ready acceptance, respect, understanding and forgiveness. The church was seen as being called to be an open and inclusive community, a calling which had often been left unanswered. This is evidenced in the continuing national and local struggle between being a guardian of the faith and being the gathering place for all God's children:

It is the tightrope between faith and order on the one hand, and openness to all those who would worship and serve on the other that the church finds itself having to negotiate. The Church of Scotland, as national church, and therefore parish church in every locality, perhaps feels this more than any other denomination in Scotland.

The church is also seen as, at its best, a model human community which positions itself at the centre of actual human community. From this comes the role of the church in nurturing the human community beyond itself; it is a critical and distinctive role: 'The church is engaged, in its internal life as well as in its mission, in the continual building of trust, support and understanding among all people.' The report goes on, then, to expect of society that anticipation of true community which is the expectation of the church – the flavour which the church is called to be for the community in which it is set:

> Any community must incorporate among all its members a recognition of mutual responsibility. In the provisional or developing human community there must be a bias towards those who are disadvantaged. Without such bias at the provisional stage the mature stage can never be attained.

It is therefore in the context of community that church, society and indeed government need to be understood, for they are all interrelated and interdependent. The Church and Nation Committee's view of its work becomes much clearer in this context – it looks from the centre of human society because that is where it is situated, holding together the real and the ideal and trying to map a way from the one to the other which all can travel together.

Because of this, the contextual community is always important. How are we to see the competing claims of different sections of society? How are we to balance, as the Committee was once asked to do, the claims to work of those in Rosyth dockyards with the demands of peace that reliance on nuclear weaponry be reduced and then eliminated? How was the Committee to compare the cries of the persecuted in Kosovo with the cries of the bombed in Serbia? Inevitably, there are times when questions need to be asked without answers being offered; there are occasions when the straightforward provision of information is all that can be expected. But through all of this is the thread of a church which places itself where the cries can be heard, where the view is of those to whom God's bias is turned, where there is the best chance to be the flavour which God imparts. This is an inclusive and open ecclesiology which leads to a social theology which places community centre stage.

Alison Elliot, convener from 1996 to 2000, spoke in Geneva in 1996 on the theme of 'A Community of Generosity'. Generosity, she said, was the hallmark of the community to which we aspire. In 1996, and still in the early years of the twenty-first century, that theme of generosity is applied to the regulations concerning how we receive and respond to refugees and asylum-seekers; it could equally well be applied to our treatment of those who suffer from disabilities or simple joblessness. It can be contrasted with the desperation into which the national lottery taps. It can certainly be the cornerstone of our thinking on wealth, its distribution and re-distribution. The community of generosity, says Alison Elliot, is a secure, trusting and confident community. The Church and Nation Committee sees it not only as a destination for which to strive but also as the way of God lived by Jesus of Nazareth and available to human society as its way also.

The Board of Social Responsibility

The Board is the inheritor of the 1869 'Committee for Christian Life and Work'. Its constitution reminds us that it has since continued and assumed

> the responsibilities, functions and interests of the Com-
> mittees on Social Service and on Moral Welfare, the
> Women's Committee on Social and Moral Welfare, and
> the Women's Council, and all other bodies (the Board's
> Constituent Bodies) which from time to time have amal-
> gamated to form the Board.

As part of its remit, the Board is charged 'to study and present essential Christian judgments on social, moral and ethical issues arising within the area of the Board's concern'. This has led in recent years to reports on such matters as human sexuality, euthanasia, human genetics and family matters. The normal pattern has been with these reports that the Board will produce only one in any given year, with each report being as a result a lengthy one. The remits to the Committee on Church and Nation and the Board of Social Responsibility have an inevitable degree of overlap: matters in the life of the nation which have moral or spiritual content would tend to include Christian judgments on social, moral and ethical issues. The phrase which has therefore proved to be important is 'arising within the area of the Board's concern'. This is to be interpreted as referring to matters which come to the attention of the Board in its social-work activities and, because these have been expanding, so has the area in which the Board is able to comment. Thus the Board's work with drug addiction led it to examine a wide range of issues to do with drugs and their use, misuse and abuse. The recommendation that a Royal Commission be established to examine the 'decriminalisation' of certain drugs came out of this context.

A history leading out of moral welfare committees is clear when other reports of the Board are highlighted. There is a whole series of reports to do with sex and related matters: reports on abortion, prostitution, human sexuality, embryology and genetics. The suitable context of sexual expression, the artificial assistance of conception, the artificial prevention of birth and the screening or modification of future generations are included here. If the Church and Nation Committee could be argued to be concerned with the kind of society in which we live, the framework within which communities are formed and thrive, the Board of Social Responsibility might be seen as concerning itself with the choices people make within such a framework. The growth in the Board's counselling services would bear witness to such an approach as well as providing the Board with an agenda for future studies.

The theme of community was important in looking at the work of the Church and Nation Committee. It expressed an ecclesiology which takes in all those people for whom the Church of Scotland has a responsibility of care – which is everyone in Scotland. And the theme returns in looking at the Board of Social Responsibility. The Board is set up to provide care for all those who come asking; it is equally true that it is at all times clear and 'up front' that this provision is undertaken 'in Christ's name' *as* the church. What we see is the community of the church serving the community at large, but a clear distinction between the two. The Board serves both as *care* and as *witness*. Because of this, there is a concern to make sure that the witness is appropriate. Thus in the 1999 report on abortion we find:

> The challenge for the church is that it is seen as irrelevant to people's lives and that it is judgmental: people are not turning to the clergy at times of distress and this is a serious issue that the church must address.

This distinction between the community of the church and the community of the world is expressed by the Board in the 1996 report on embryology:

> In everyday life . . . we are continually faced by a conflict of obligations. As Christians we are met by the challenge of the Gospel and the Kingdom of God. Yet we live in a fallen, sinful world. No matter how much we pray and

strive that his Kingdom come, his will be done on earth as it is in heaven, this world does not as yet recognise God's rule. It never will until Jesus comes at the last, finally to cleanse away all evil, and transform all things so that they become his renewed and perfect creation. Meantime, we grapple with the task of relating divine ideal to imperfect reality, and are caught in the tension between affirming those norms which God has revealed in His Word and through Christ, such as the sanctity of human life, and applying them to the exigencies of human need and circumstance.

There is to be found here a theology of '*a city set on a hill*' which can be contrasted with the '*salt and leaven*' approach detectable in the work of the Church and Nation Committee. Both are biblical approaches to social theology, and each represents a particular ecclesiology.

The Church: in, of or for the World?

Will Storrar has spoken of models of church and nation, picking up from Richard Niebuhr and Robert Webber.[4] Webber's typology speaks of identifying models, separating models and transforming models. In the first, the church participates in the structures of life through compromise with the prevailing culture or at least through a recognition of the tension with culture. In the second, the church withdraws itself entirely or sets itself up as a counter-culture. In the third, the church believes in the alteration of the structures of life either now or as the ultimate goal of history. Storrar examines these three in terms whereby the first model is seen in the medieval Catholic vision of Scotland, the second is found in much of the Reformation tradition in Scotland, and the third is located in modern secular thought. He admits, however, as we all must, that it is not quite that easy to distil complex social movements and world-views. All

of them are something of a mixture, and all of them
have their pluses and their minuses. From the point of
view of our present discussion, we can say that the
Church and Nation Committee has operated mostly
within the parameters of the first and third models, while
the Board of Social Responsibility has tended more
towards the second.

Church and Nation works assiduously to maintain
good relations with numerous other bodies in 'civil
society'. Thus, for example, the Refugee Council,
Amnesty International, the Poverty Alliance, the trade
unions and even political parties are a regular part of
the Committee's work of 'networking', maintaining
contact with a nation and its structures. This fits in very
well with the view of a national church which carries
responsibility for all the citizens; the church seeks to
identify with the nation in which it is set, to work
alongside these other bodies to promote the common
good. The good of the nation as a whole is sought
through a critical engagement with those individuals and
organisations in a position to effect change for better or
worse. This engagement, this identification with the
condition of the nation, is aimed at bringing the Gospel
to bear at the heart of the life of the nation in a way
which would not be possible if the church were set or
set itself on the sidelines. Only in this way, it is argued,
can the transformation of structures be achieved.

The Board of Social Responsibility has tended to come
at things from another angle, which is more one of
distinctiveness than of identification. Its work of social
care has emphasised that here is something different;
and this has resulted, because of employment policies,
in a long-running dispute with the Equal Opportunities
Commission. If the Church and Nation Committee's
ethical language has tended to be consequentialist or

teleological, the Board has been more likely to be deontological.

Will Storrar argues persuasively that another model is needed, and that this is an incarnational model. At its best, the church already works on this model in both the bodies discussed so far. It is a model which builds on the solidarity lived by Jesus of Nazareth, a solidarity which affirms, calls away and transforms as circumstances demand. As a model it seeks, like the Church of Scotland itself, to have the best of all possible worlds. Such a model does, of course, require the work undertaken to be earthed and embodied. The Justice and Peace Commission of the Roman Catholic church provides a way for issues of social justice to be discussed and acted upon locally, the kind of network of local groups which would be invaluable to the Church and Nation Committee. The social-care aspects of the work of the Board of Social Responsibility allow a local involvement through support and friends' groups embodying the commitment of the church to those whom society might prefer to forget. It is, of course, possible that the incarnation of the Kingdom's values can be lived out in the life of the world without ever being recognised as such – we only have to read the prologue to John's Gospel to discover that.

This is where the methodology of social thinking in the church needs to be examined. There is a pressing need for Christians locally to become far more involved, in a way that connects them with others in their own denomination and with those of other denominations, in discussing and learning about the intersection of our faith and the world in which we are set. The centrality of faith to the world tends to be rather more widely accepted in congregations than is the centrality of the world to faith. The Church of Scotland is often criticised (most often from within) for its preponderance of committees, its bureaucratic structure. This is because so many feel disconnected from that structure and the work it seeks to accomplish. Primarily, that work aims to give church members the information and the analytical tools to help them deal with such information. It is to those who have traditionally carried the teaching office within the church (the parish ministers) that the task most often falls of engaging those entrusted to their care in this wider discussion and debate on social and political matters. It may be that a methodology needs to be explored which will bring the wider church, prepared and equipped, into the discussion in advance of rather than in the wake of the General Assembly of the Church of Scotland. In this way, the search for the best of all possible worlds might reach the top of the church's agenda – an agenda with mass participation.

The final question for us and indeed for the church, therefore, is this: if the church really is to seek the best of all possible worlds, then *for whom*? If the development of liberation theology has taught us nothing else, it has taught us to ask questions about who benefits. It has taught us to be suspicious of anything which purports to benefit everyone. Thus the Church and Nation Committee joined with the Board of World Mission in becoming involved in the 'WTO Alliance', a group of organisations profoundly concerned that the World Trade Organisation's claims (for example, that further liberalisation of trade makes everyone winners) are a cover for the further exploitation of the poor countries of the world by rich multinational companies and a way of taking control over the basics of life even further away from the already powerless.

In essence, this act of suspicion is based on the biblical doctrine of sin. It presumes that power corrupts and that those who are powerless will be the victims of this corruption. Suspicion is thus an act of solidarity which places the church on the side of the poor and the powerless. The Priority Areas Fund of the Board of National Mission (now incorporated into the Scottish Churches Community Trust) has added to much practical work being achieved by the Board of Social Responsibility and theoretical work undertaken by the Church and Nation Committee in setting the work of the church appropriately alongside the poor. It is important to look at what this says: it does not say, for example, that poor and powerless people are intrinsically better people; it says nothing about their personal generosity or wisdom or morals. What it does say is that the place of the church is where Jesus of Nazareth chose to be – with the dispossessed, seeing what they see, enduring what they endure, hoping for what is their hope. And this is because the poor have the privilege of seeing most clearly the points at which society hurts its members, damages the hopes of its people, and falls short of the vision of the kingdom.

The theological reflection arising from that process is embarked upon anew with every new project. The spoken or written theology handed down from the past in witness and in hope is given flesh anew. Transformation is hoped for anew in every new incarnation of present witness and hope, transformation which, as Will Storrar reminds us, has not been achieved by the history of the church of Jesus Christ in Scotland. His response is to call us to contrition:

the kind of contrition which Anthony Ross called for in 1970, a contrition for the failure of the Christian Church to re-shape Scottish society in the light of the Gospel. And contrition can bring not only forgiveness but a new clarity of thought after the removal of old visions now turned into deceptive illusions.[5]

At times in its history, the church has identified with the power structures of our land and has thus separated itself from the poor and the powerless. We are being taught from other parts of the world that joy and transformation, not only of the society but also of the church, is to be found in an identification with the margins. In these days, the social theology of the Church of Scotland is in a position to build on the various traditions of identification and separation and turn the shortcomings of the past into a vision for the future.

Placed *in* this land, made up *of* its people, it can be the church *for* Scotland. It can be the body of Christ, following Jesus of Nazareth, God's incarnate Word, to say: *I am for you.* Our failures require humility of us; but faith sustains our hope.

Notes

1. Professor John Baillie chaired a 'Commission for the Interpretation of God's Will in the Present Crisis' from 1940 to 1946. The reports of 1941 to 1945 were brought together in 1946 under the title: *God's Will for Church and Nation.*
2. This list of issues is taken from William Storrar's account, 'Liberating the Kirk' in *God's Will in a Time of Crisis*, ed. Andrew R. Morton, CTPI, 1994.
3. Andrew McLellan was speaking at the same conference and is published in the same volume as William Storrar.
4. *Scottish Identity*, Edinburgh, 1990, pp. 155f.
5. *Scottish Identity*, 1990, p. 161.

I sit with my back to the future, watching
time pouring away into the past. I sit being helplessly
lugged backwards
through the Debatable Land of history, listening
to the execrations, the scattered cries, the falling of
    roof-trees
in the lamentable dark.

Norman MacCaig, from *Crossing the Border*

12

An Evangelical Alliance
Approach to Social Theology

Jeremy Balfour

A major challenge facing Christians in the twenty-first century has to do with truth and tolerance in the public arena. In the face of secular and pluralistic society structures increasingly antipathetic to the Christian world-view, the Evangelical Alliance does not accept that Christians should retreat into a sectarian inwardness or ghetto mentality. Rather, like the Reformists, it regards the church's main task as involving the transformation of society. This approach claims that 'being' the church involves preserving its God-given distinctiveness while simultaneously engaging in a meaningful way with 'the powers that be' and where necessary confronting them. In this regard, it has recently published *Uniting for Change: An Evangelical Vision for Transforming Society*, which sets out the rationale for its vision as a movement for change rooted in a contemporary understanding of the Kingdom of God at work in society.

John Stott has highlighted the need for Christians to develop a 'Christian mind . . . which can think with Christian integrity about the problems of the contemporary world'.[1] This points to the fact that evangelicals, apart from a few commendable exceptions, have not been noted for seriously engaging at a scholarly or practical level with contemporary issues. The reasons for this are manifold, but have included fears concerning the social gospel, liberal dilution of biblical truth, 'surrender' to the world, and even fundamental questioning about whether Christians should engage with the world at all.

But, through *Uniting for Change*, the Alliance reflects something of a recent general and positive trend for evangelicals to address public issues in a more considered and constructive way. *Uniting for Change* is also about practical social engagement at the grassroots. Evangelicals in general have been unwilling to engage in the social gospel and have not taken a holistic view of mission. Over the last few years, this has been changing, and projects such as Bethany Christian Trust in Edinburgh and Glasgow City Mission have started to awaken evangelical engagement.

Evangelical Alliance and Care have tried to engage in the political process as well. Rather than shouting from the touchline, they sought interaction with politicians in a constructive way. When the parliament in Scotland was reformed in 1999, both organisations appointed parliamentary officers to engage with MSPs, civil servants and the wider civic society. Part of their role is to encourage and persuade evangelicals to take part in the political process.

Of course, many new moral and socio-political issues, such as bioethics and human rights, are not just controversial public issues. Christians frequently disagree with each other on how to respond, and dispute to what extent the Bible or tradition might contribute to debate. Christians have often been more used to speaking to each other than to society, and the task of interpreting the Bible and evangelical concerns in the public realm remains a pressing one if evangelicals wish to be understood and so progress their declared transformational role.

Evangelicals have rightly been identified by their commitment to the Scriptures as the rule for life and faith, and in this regard it must be stated at once that the Alliance remains committed to the pre-eminence of the Bible in the process of social theology and ethical decision-making. However, Kevin Vanhoozer has been one of the new breed of thoughtful evangelicals who has recently helped to show that biblical truth is properly multidimensional and that contextualised theological truth belongs to the realm of discourse:

> There may ... be several normative points of view in the Bible that are all authoritative because they disclose aspects of the truth. It is therefore possible simultaneously to admit a multiplicity of perspectives and to maintain an 'aspectival' realism.[2]

In this article, Vanhoozer presses the case for dialogue in the task of evangelical theologising, not so that in some post-modern sense meaning ceases to be definitive, but so that biblical authority is maintained while account is simultaneously taken of Scripture's 'multiplicity of theologies' and time-honoured denominational hermen-eutical traditions. Allied to a commitment to the primary yet more open and deeper use of Scripture in the cause of responsible exegesis, as a guard against subjective relativism there is increasing recognition that the theological and ethical task involves insightful input also from the spheres of tradition, experience, reason and scientific fact.[3] This does not mean that all interpretations are equally valid, but that collaborative theology done from a variety of perspectives is able to produce a rich and academically respected consensus or collegiality, which is nevertheless no mere compromise of truth.[4]

As in purely doctrinal issues, so also with an evangelical approach to applied social theology. The Evangelical Alliance's Millennium Manifesto incorporated a decision to create a Policy Commission, which was initiated in 1999. Its remit was to identify contemporary controversial issues, commission relevant studies, and, in adopting an evangelical viewpoint, recommend appropriate policy statements. The issues with which it was primarily to be concerned were to be typically of an ethical nature with societal, national or international implications – as distinct from purely theological and doctrinal concerns. With a strong educational objective and addressed primarily to evangelical Christians and churches, its studies were intended to be of wider application and relevance to the Christian community, but also society at large, as it sought to offer a co-ordinated response to matters of wider public debate.

The Policy Commission functions as a steering group to the Evangelical Alliance, comprising evangelical representatives from a wide range of academic, scientific and professional disciplines. Its reports, containing summarised Alliance affirmations and recommendations, are produced following a wide-ranging discussion and consultation process, both internally through the Evangelical Alliance membership, and externally with reference to appropriately qualified academics and practitioners in the relevant fields. Its studies are therefore multi-disciplinary and multiperspectival. Its process could, perhaps, most accurately be classified as 'study-dialogue' methodology. Although the majority of contributors are themselves evangelicals, they are not afraid to interact with scholars and experts from other traditions and faith (or indeed non-faith) sectors.

The Commission's first two studies, which have received wide acclaim and been extensively employed in real-life situations, covered the important contemporary issues of transsexuality and GM crops and foods.[5] Transsexuality is a highly controversial subject, surrounded by its own mythology, involving far-reaching consequences for society as a whole. Little prior published material existed, and Christian awareness was virtually nil. The report produced by the multidisciplinary working group formed the basis for a submission to the government's consultation on birth certificates, and to date has played a crucial role in the debate concerning recognition of transsexual rights to gender self-determination. It was peer-reviewed and commended for its scientific accuracy, ethical judgment, theological relevance and humanity. Not only has the study proved invaluable to churches and pastoral workers, but it has been used extensively by public bodies and other faith groups to inform themselves concerning a difficult and complex issue. Taken seriously by the academic world, it has directly provoked considerable debate in scholarly journals and elsewhere in the public sphere.

GM crops and foods is an important contemporary issue on which Christians themselves are divided. The Alliance study, undertaken in a fruitful partnership with the Church of Scotland, sought to examine the scientific, ethical, agricultural, economic and theological cases for and against GM. It was able, through a process of managed dialogue and peer review, to produce a balanced and considered treatment of the subject together with an assessment of the implications of GM. The Alliance Council received the report and, armed with an in-depth analysis, had available the resources to formulate an informed series of affirmations which it believed characterised an evangelical response to the issues. The report has received appreciative critical review and has spearheaded an up-to-date Christian response to environmental concerns which are particularly apposite in the light of the hugely significant 2002 Earth Summit.

The next report to appear from the Policy Commission will consider the subject of relationship between Nation and Faith in the twenty-first century. Examining the critical issues involved in the future of evangelical Christianity within a pluralist, secularist and rapidly changing political and public context, this study will seek to lead public debate on such questions as church and state, monarchy and interfaith grouping in public life. To produce a credible outcome, such a study requires special considerations. Accordingly, a commission of enquiry incorporating a cross-section of perspectives and representative bodies of opinion has been assembled and will invite and consider evidence in the format of a parliamentary select committee, publishing evidence and responses as it proceeds. The objective will be to lead, inform and educate the Evangelical Alliance constituency concerning these unavoidable issues, while (it is hoped) leading a debate on contributing a respected and credible voice within society itself from a Christian perspective.

During the nineteenth century, evangelical Christians led the way with regard to social change. This process has been lost for nearly 100 years. At last, evangelicals from all denominations are waking up to the challenges and opportunities of social theology in Scotland today. There is a long way still to go, and many evangelicals still need to be persuaded that they should be involved. Evangelical Alliance south of the border is further down the road, but at least the debate has started here in Scotland.

Notes

1. *New Issues Facing Christians Today*, London: Marshall Pickering, 1999, p. 36.
2. 'The Voice and the Actor', in John G. Stackhouse Jr, ed., *Evangelical Futures*, Leicester: Apollos, 2000, pp. 78–9.
3. See J. Philip Wogaman, *Christian Ethics: A Historical Introduction*, Louisville: Westminster/John Knox Press, 1993, p. 278.
4. For discussion of the Evangelical Alliance's approach to doctrinal issues through its Commission on Unity and Truth among Evangelicals (ACUTE), see David Hilborn, 'Truth, Collegiality and Consensus: The Dynamics of an Evangelical Theological Commission', in *Evangelical Review of Theology* 26:1 (2002), 23–44.
5. Don Horrocks, ed., *Transsexuality*, Carlisle: Paternoster, 2000; Donald Bruce and Don Horrocks, eds, *Modifying Creation? GM Crops and Foods: A Christian Perspective*, Carlisle: Paternoster, 2001.

cailèideascop-Dhia
beò-dhathan dian-loisgeach

kaleidoscope-God
conflagration of living colours

uile-ghlòrmhorachd
na chaoir-bhuidealaich

all-gloriousness
ablaze

solas dreòsach neo-bhàsmhor
a' spreadhadh tro phriosm nan dùl

incandescent immortal light
exploding through the elemental prism

bogha-froise drìlseach na shìneadh
o bhithbhuantachd gu bithbhuantachd

effulgent rainbow spanning
from everlasting to everlasting

sàr-iomlanachd sheachdfhillte
sìorraidheachd shruthshoillseach

sevenfold absolute perfection
fluorescent infinitude

rinneadh na h-uile dhathan leat agus às
d' eugmhais cha d' rinneadh aon dath a rinneadh

all colours were made by you
and without you was no colour made that was made

Fearghas MacFhionnlaigh,
from *A Hymn which is not to Lenin*,
translated from the Gaelic,
Laoidh nach eil do Lenin, by the author

13

An Iona Community Perspective

Norman Shanks

Since its foundation in 1938, the Iona Community has had a wholehearted commitment to the theological task. There is still debate about George MacLeod's own stature as a theologian: while his books were certainly limited, his distinctive perspective, enriched by insights and influences from many different traditions – Protestant and Catholic, Celtic and Orthodox – is evident in his powerful pamphlets and *Coracle* articles, his memorable sermons and the soaring poetry of his prayers. The general view within the Community is still that Ralph Morton, George MacLeod's deputy leader from 1951 to 1967, was probably a theologian of greater significance and substance, pioneer of the lay training movement, author for instance of *God's Frozen People* and *The Household of Faith*. Among the membership since the early days, there have always been some people whose theological contribution has been especially recognised; and, while it is invidious to pick out anyone from the present members, the name of Ian Fraser must be mentioned, author of *Doing Theology – the People's Work*, dean of mission at Selly Oak Colleges following a period on the World Council of Churches staff, still in his eighties travelling and consulting widely in the field of basic Christian communities.

The Community's theology, and its perception of what the theological task constitutes, has always been directly related to its fundamental commitment to mission – to seeking 'new ways to touch the hearts of all' (as one of the Community's favourite prayers puts it), to rebuilding the common life, to contributing to the renewal of church and society. The particular approach to theology tends to be characterised as 'incarnational'; it is rooted in the reality of 'the Word made flesh', grounded in a personal obedience to Christ that is deepened and enriched through being worked out within a social setting and a framework of communal accountability, dependent on the conviction, essential alike to both the Celtic and Benedictine traditions, that God is 'in the midst' of every aspect of life. Equally, though, the Community's theology may be regarded as 'biblical' (valuing the tradition of Scripture and the challenging insights and rich themes it contains), 'orthodox' (thoroughly trinitarian, if not necessarily in the full-blown classical sense), 'radical' (in the sense of both looking back respectfully whence we have come and facing up to the cutting-edge issues of present and future), 'liberal' (in the openness, the inclusiveness, the spirit of exploration that does not pretend to have all the answers) and 'contextual' (emerging from and relevant to the specific circumstances).

And the incarnational approach to theology both leads to and cannot be separated from the commitment to an integrated understanding of spirituality – linking work and worship, faith and political action, seeing the whole of life as spiritual, discerning the presence of God in 'every blessed thing'. The life of the Community expresses the conviction that authentic spirituality is not escapist but engaged. There must be an emphasis on the 'down-to-earthness' of God, the everyday alongside the eternal, the communal action alongside the solitary contemplation. Contrary to the too-frequent presentation of a detached, sanitised and romanticised type of 'Celtic spirituality', God is to be experienced and encountered not only in remote, beautiful and tranquil places but also in human relationships and in struggling with the issues of the day. As one of the Community's staff once said, 'People come to Iona for peace and quiet and go away looking for peace and justice!'

The Community's commitment to 'social theology' is reflected not only in the engagement with political issues and the commitment to social renewal but also in the communal setting where the theology happens. One of George MacLeod's best-remembered sayings was 'only a demanding common task builds community'. For many of us, 'doing social theology' would seem a much too grandiose and pretentious description of our common life and activities. The theological processes are seldom self-conscious or deliberate: we are unlikely to set apart time in our meetings for theological reflection specifically – as we do for worship, which is the beginning and end of all our activities. Rather, the theology – the 'God-talk' – flows in and out of the discussion naturally, in the exploration of the purposes and promise of God, the vision and the values of the kingdom and our shared calling to witness and service in our own context.

Above all, the Community's 'social theology' is evident in the Rule, that reflects and sums up the Community's aims and activities and binds the members together within a framework of mutual accountability. The Rule is a discipline that is both individual and corporate. It has five elements which have a seamless interconnectedness – a daily devotional discipline, an economic discipline involving the sharing of money and a commitment to tithing (for the work of the church and other concerns as well as for the Community), commitments to use time in a way that is planned and balanced, to meet together regularly (this happens in monthly local 'Family Groups' and four plenary meetings each year: this is where the theology is done, in engaging before God and with one another to discuss the issues of the day, to challenge and support one another, to worship together and to celebrate our common life), and commitment to action for justice and peace, through involvement in political activity and movements for social change.

'Doing social theology' is not an exercise that is particular to the Iona Community or any other group or organisation. It is the pilgrimage that is shared by all those who seek to walk in the way of Jesus Christ, to respond in faith to the issues around us, and to do so not just on our own as a matter of individual obedience but together, benefiting from one another's insight, experience and support. The important themes facing the churches today – the future shape and witness of the church, the challenge to mission in today's world, how our faith relates to social policies and political priorities – are concerns that have been integral to the life of the Community since our foundation over sixty years ago, and remain fundamental to all that we do today.

We certainly do not claim to have all the answers, and we are conscious that in our work, often at the frontiers of mission, we do not always get it right! But we are immensely encouraged at the response to our concerns and activities, embodied not only in the experience of the common life shared, through worship, work, discussion and social events, by the guests and staff at our residential centres on Iona and at Camas on Mull, and in our mainland work – in the fields of worship, youth and publications – but also in what our members are doing through their work and other activities in their own local situations. It is a source of great encouragement and strength that more and more people, it would seem, throughout Britain and overseas too, are interested in what we are doing and saying, and want to become involved in and identify with the life and work of the Community. There may be some pointers here to the way forward for the churches more generally – indicating how important it is that Gospel witness should be rooted in corporate worship and a personal devotional discipline; how significant the ecumenical dimension is to the way of discipleship today; and how, in dealing with the deep questions of meaning and purpose that so many people are asking in trying to make sense of this complex and confusing world in which we live, there is a compelling appeal in an engaged approach to spirituality – that sees social and political action as essential to the Christian way.

For some time, I have been impressed by some of the insights in a book called *Resident Aliens*, by the Americans Stanley Hauerwas and W. H. Willimon. They called on the church, and on each Christian community – whether a local congregation or the Iona Community – to fulfil its vocation as a committed 'community of the cross' rather than becoming a compromised 'conspiracy of cordiality'. We discover and experience fullness of life not by seeking to survive at all costs, with a steadfast resistance to change, but by being ready to take risks for the sake of God's kingdom, to live out the divine virtues of hospitality and solidarity, by reaching out in ways that are welcoming, open and inclusive, by standing alongside those who are marginalised, oppressed and discriminated against – on account of their race, their gender, their orientation, their poverty.

That is why the commitment to justice and peace is so important to the Iona Community's life together – why we are involved in the campaign against the arms trade, why we are at Faslane protesting against Trident, why we are committed to Jubilee Scotland and the movement against the World Trade Organisation's latest proposals, why we place such priority on racial justice and the reform of nationality law, why we are giving increased attention to environmental concerns, why we are totally opposed to sectarianism – a running sore within Scottish society whose insidious influence on our attitudes and culture is so deep and damaging. We hope that the voice of the church will be raised more strongly against every movement and viewpoint that oppresses and marginalises, that the life and priorities of the churches will be geared towards rooting out and changing all that is divisive and contrary to God's reconciling purpose for our world.

Doing social theology in this fashion is no easy option. The process can be difficult, and, as is almost inevitable when living on the edge of risk, there will be setbacks and disappointments. But it is also immensely energising and enriching although, as well as commitment, it demands a degree of resilience and persistence – the Columban gifts of 'courage, faith and cheerfulness' of which one of the Community's prayers speaks!

Further reading

Chasing the Wild Goose: the story of the Iona Community (revised edition), Ron Ferguson, Wild Goose Publications, 1998.

Iona – God's Energy: the vision and spirituality of the Iona Community, Norman Shanks, Hodder & Stoughton, 1999.

Further information from:

The Iona Community, Pearce Institute, 840 Govan Road, Glasgow G51 3UU. Tel. 0141–445 4561; www.iona.org.uk

leatsa dathan a' chosmais

yours the colours of the cosmos

na solais-bhliadhnaichean air fad mar
phlathadh-seòid do lùdaig-fhàinne

the sum-total of all light years but
a jewel-gleam of your pinkie ring

leatsa dathan na talmhainn

yours the colours of the earth

Niagara a' tàirneanach san oidhche
is tuil-sholais oirre

floodlit Niagara
thundering in the night

drùchdan drìthleannach sa mhadainn
a' crithinn air lìon damhain-allaidh

iridescent morning dewdrop
trembling on a web

Fearghas MacFhionnlaigh,
from *A Hymn which is not to Lenin*,
translated from the Gaelic,
Laoidh nach eil do Lenin, by the author

14

Theology of Insistence

An Ecumenical Perspective

Alastair Hulbert

Although Visser 't Hooft, the first General Secretary of the World Council of Churches (WCC), actively supported the creation of an ecumenical body to represent the churches in relation to the European Communities in Brussels, it took some thirty years, until the mid-1990s, for the WCC to arrange a visit to find out what was going on. Of course, the Cold War had ended in the meantime. The European Ecumenical Commission for Church and Society (EECC), as it was by then called, had changed and was going to change a lot more: no longer just Western European churches in relation to the Western European institutions, but a broadening ecumenism preparing to join forces with the pan-European Conference of European Churches and looking to include in its mission political institutions beyond the European Union and the Council of Europe.

Theology in Eastern Europe during these years was done under communism and was in many cases based on resistance, a theology of resistance. A significant exception was to be found in Prague with the Christian Peace Conference which Joséf Hromadka founded in the 1950s, developing a dialogue between Christians and Marxists. But after Hromadka's death at the end of the

1960s (some say of a broken heart at the Warsaw Pact's repression of the Prague Spring), the Christian Peace Conference's dialogue with power became increasingly discredited, not least by Czechs themselves. It was a tragedy that Hromadka's brand of theology and dialogue was snuffed out by events. In 1977, several Czech theologians, ministers and lay persons were among those who founded Charter 77. Inspired by the Helsinki accords, this was a rallying point demanding of the Czech government that a whole range of human rights be respected. Many of the chartists, notably Václav Havel, suffered harassment and imprisonment for their witness to the truth and their resistance to the regime.

In Western Europe during the post-war years – in Germany, Switzerland, England, Scotland and elsewhere – another important theological development was taking place. This was in the field of industrial mission. In Scotland, a pioneer in the field was Rev. Cameron Wallace, industrial chaplain to the shipyards in the lower reaches of the Clyde. His was a patient, long-term approach to industrial institutions in terms of presence, trust, dialogue, mediation, arbitration; in relation to workers, their families, shop stewards and trade unions, management and owners. (We can note in passing that the Catholic worker-priest theology, based on words like *enracinement*, naturalisation and incarnation, was another remarkable twentieth-century theology also in the field of industrial mission, having much in common with Dietrich Bonhoeffer's prison theology.) Unsurprisingly, those involved in such new forms of mission to the structures of society often had considerable difficulty in convincing the institutional churches of their validity and importance.

In the 1970s and 1980s, something else was happening as well, not least in Brussels. It was recognised in the report of the WCC Assembly in 1991 in Canberra in these words: 'There is an urgent need today for a new type of mission, not into foreign lands but into "foreign" structures. By this term we mean economic, social and political structures, which do not at all conform to Christian moral standards.' Bishop Lesslie Newbigin made a similar point in a lecture at Carberry in 1993, his last in Scotland before his death, when he spoke of three types of mission: mission to individuals, mission to structures and mission to ideologies. EECCS, over the years, was involved in mission to the structures, and also, though to a lesser extent, mission to ideologies. (How often EECCS was assumed to be a simple chaplaincy to the European civil servants, corresponding to mission to individuals!)

Back to the WCC visit to EECCS in 1995, mentioned above. There were about twenty guests from all over the world. Following a hard day discussing EU policy with civil servants and commissioners in small informal groups all over Brussels, we had dinner together in the Ecumenical Centre and then moved on to discuss and reflect about the day's events. After a while, one of the group, Marshall Fernando, a layman from Sri Lanka, stood up and said that he had never understood what EECCS was all about until now. But what had become clear to him during the day was that EECCS was involved in a *theology of insistence*, which contrasted with the *theology of resistance* which he had known in different forms in Asia or under communism in Eastern Europe and fascism in Latin America. He could find no better way of describing the theology which undergirded the mission of dialogue with the institutions that he had just experienced.

Marc Lenders was the original staff member of EECCS, there at its launch and serving it for more than thirty years. For over twenty years, the relationship of EECCS to the European Commission which Marc worked with was informal and tenuous. It depended on an ecumenical association of civil servants and individual officials who supported its work and vocation. It was only in 1990, following a successful working visit of senior representatives of the member churches of EECCS to the European Commission, that President Jacques Delors, who hosted the visit, opened the door to a more formal relationship. Of course it couldn't be formal in the political sense, there being no basis in the treaties for dialogue between the European Commission and the churches. But official dialogue is what effectively began at that time, and has continued in conference form ever since, surviving two changes in the presidency. Typically, an agenda would be agreed between EECCS and the Forward Studies Unit (the Commission think-tank close to the President). It might be agriculture, work and unemployment, sustainable development, enlargement of the Union, the future of north–south relations. The churches would nominate specialists in the subject to be discussed, while the Commission would be repre-sented by specialist civil servants, occasionally an MEP, sometimes an ambassador. The meeting itself, which would last for a day, would take place in one of the Commission's meeting rooms with interpreters.

Marc Lenders' guidelines on how to conduct dialogue with international institutions are an important reference for such relations with the European institutions, a practical theological tool.

1. Be part of a constituency;
2. Be expert in the subject-matter (know more than they do);
3. Have an overall view (global analysis);

4. Focus on doubts, on impasses, on the need for new ideas;

5. Be financially independent from the institutions with which you are talking;

6. Have a diversified strategy to cope with different situations, and choose one or two approaches;

7. Enter into a *process* of dialogue (ad hoc contacts bear little lasting fruit);

8. Prepare for this dialogue work with the help of sociologists competent in the relevant methodology.

These guidelines supply the necessary preconditions for dialogue. They do not, however, pretend to give a full description of what such dialogue should mean for Christians engaged in mission to the structures. If the churches are doing no more than politics or economics as such, however competent or specialist their contribution, there is no particular reason for them to be engaged as churches. Yet, at the same time, to see the dialogue as a debate about ethics and moral values, which is a commonly voiced perception of the European officials themselves, is also problematic. In the atmosphere of the quite unexpected collapse of the Soviet Union and the impending completion of the single market, ethics and values seemed attractive concepts even in as secular a 'state' as the European Union. But what do they mean in such a vast economic culture? Commenting on a Forward Studies Unit document of the time entitled *The Vocation of Europe*, Lesslie Newbigin wrote:

> It is . . . one of the sure signs of a culture in terminal decline when it begins to talk about the need for moral values . . . We cannot decide to 'have a new economic system' or 'promote morality' simply because these would be desirable.

These things cannot be detached from the total belief-system which governs public life.

So, what is the theological basis of the churches' dialogue? A theology of insistence indicates how the dialogue should happen, its urgency and commitment. It speaks of the methodology of missionary dialogue. The substance of the theology is multiple, each element being unpacked as the particular subject of dialogue in question makes it necessary: theology of creation for dialogue with the Commission on its environmental or energy or transport policy, feminist theology or theology of the poor for dialogue on social policy, and so on.

EECCS, now the Church and Society Commission of the Conference of European Churches, has a large metaphorical carpet bag filled with international ecumenical theology to draw on for its theology of insistence. It's an exciting but intimidating task, as intimidating perhaps as God's call to Jonah, which scared him out of his wits at the idea of preaching to the European Union of the time. In the end, it is God's own insistence which wins the day. 'And should not I pity Nineveh, that great city, in which there are more than 120,000 persons who do not know their right hand from their left, and also much cattle?'

It's comforting to know that the CAP is included too!

leatsa dathan an danns
fir-chlis is stròb-sholas

yours the colours of dance
aurora borealis and strobe

leatsa dathan a' ghaoil
coinfèataidh air sìoda geal

yours the colours of love
confetti on white silk

leatsa dathan na gàire
cleasan-teine is sùilean cloinne

yours the colours of laughter
fireworks and children's eyes

leatsa speictream na beatha
leatsa a-mhàin

yours the spectrum of life
only yours

's leinne an dubhaigeann
ma dhùnas Tu do rosgan

and ours the abyss
should Your eyelids close

Fearghas MacFhionnlaigh,
from *A Hymn which is not to Lenin*,
translated from the Gaelic,
Laoidh nach eil do Lenin, by the author